Praise for
Kingdom Man

Kingdom Man is a playbook for life. Tony Evans has laid out the game plan to follow if we, as men, want to live a championship life. He describes not only what we need to do, but more importantly, he also shows us how to do it. This book is a must-read for any man who wants to live up to God's design for male leadership of the family!

—Tony Dungy, NBC *Football Night in America* analyst

I'm a big game-plan guy, and Tony has the ability to lay out a game plan for those of us who want to be Kingdom Men. As we have gotten to know each other over the years, it's become clear to me that Tony has a heart for the Lord and a gift for communicating God's principles.

—Coach Joe Gibbs, owner, Joe Gibbs Racing

We all long to fulfill our destiny; some of us spend a lifetime trying to identify what our destiny is and what we must do to achieve it. There was a time when I thought my only destiny was to win a Super Bowl, but after reading *Kingdom Man,* I was reminded that God has more in store for all of us and that greatness is awaiting if we follow God's plan. *Kingdom Man* will allow you to focus on what you are destined for and how to achieve your destiny.

—Leslie Frazier, Minnesota Vikings head coach

Every woman wants a kingdom man. Maybe she can't find the words to describe what she's longing for, but she knows him when she sees him—the unmistakable sense of purpose, the reputation marked by integrity, the willingness to be a strong leader and tender caregiver at the same time—this is what she desires. And this is the reason every single woman should read this book: to be able to spot a man worth committing to while steering clear of his counterfeit peers. It is also why every married woman should read this book and give it to the man in her life. The man of every woman's dream is the man found in these pages. So read . . . and keep on reading until you're not only clear on what you want, but you're also clear on what you need from the man you have.

—Priscilla Shirer, Bible teacher and author

If you want to experience all that God has destined for you, *Kingdom Man* is a must-read. In it, Dr. Tony Evans gives helpful and relevant tools that you can use to bring yourself to a place of influence and impact. This book will help you progress from being a good man to being a great man!

—Tony Romo, Dallas Cowboys quarterback

In the NFL we have a saying, "Don't tell me what you can do, show me the tape!" The meaning is that the tape tells us all we need to know. When considering what it is to be a kingdom man, checking Dr. Tony Evans's tape will tell you all you need to know. He is clearly a kingdom man himself, who has raised his own sons to be kingdom men, and who has also had a positive impact on so many other men. For the last two and a half years I have been blessed by God to be able to sit under the authority of Dr. Evans as my pastor and more intimately as my discipler. This book is a must-read for any man who is tired of living beneath his purpose and wants to pursue the true greatness that God intends for him.

—Jon Kitna, Dallas Cowboys quarterback

TONY EVANS

KINGDOM MAN

EVERY MAN'S DESTINY

EVERY WOMAN'S DREAM

  TYNDALE HOUSE PUBLISHERS, INC.
CAROL STREAM, ILLINOIS

I dedicate this book to my grandsons:
Jackson
Jesse III
Jerry Jr.
Kanaan
Jude
Joel
Jonathan II
Kingdom men in the making

CONTENTS

ACKNOWLEDGMENTS

I want to express my appreciation to the excellent team at Focus on the Family and Tyndale House Publishers, Inc., for their vision and heart to see this book come into being. For the cadence among all who are dedicated to unleashing this message to kingdom men, I am grateful.

INTRODUCTION

I love the Indiana Jones movies. Who doesn't? Indiana Jones was all man. Here was this archaeologist spending countless hours, days, weeks, months, and sometimes even years in search of valuable artifacts. Of course he faced perilous obstacles along the way. Indy had difficulties, resistance, and dangers to overcome. Yet he always made it. And in the end, he always uncovered his treasure.

Along a similar line are the *National Treasure* movies, starring Nicolas Cage. Cage's character, Benjamin Franklin Gates, lived in pursuit of clues that would lead him to what he was seeking. Again, he faced danger, adversity, depravation, and even, at times, disaster. Yet everything was worth it when he, like Indiana, got the treasure.

Jesus speaks of a treasure. And He calls it the kingdom of God. He says that this kingdom is an unusually valuable treasure for which absolutely nothing should stand in the way. In eschatological terms, the kingdom refers to the millennial reign of Christ when He will return to run Earth from Jerusalem for His thousand-year reign. Yet in the here and now, the kingdom has also been set up for us through kingdom principles, covenants, responsibilities, privileges, rights, rules, ethics, coverings, and authority.

> *Jesus speaks of a treasure. And He calls it the kingdom of God.*

"The kingdom of heaven is like a treasure hidden in a field . . ." (Matthew 13:44).

A treasure is worth fighting for. A priceless treasure, like this one, is worth everything you have. But don't just take my word for it. Jesus said it himself.

The reason why so many men today are living without so much as a semblance of treasure is because they have not understood the mystery of the kingdom; instead, they settle for trinkets, gadgets, golf clubs, video games, careers, cars, and vacation packages.

Those things are okay—unless they take you off course from pursuing the kingdom.

Unless they become your goal.

My son Jonathan is a big guy. In the NFL, he's taken downs with some of the best players. He can hold his own. But he wasn't always that big. One time I remember him running up to my office at the church asking me to come down to the gym and watch his five-foot-three frame dunk the basketball. He had been practicing for months.

Once I got there, Jonathan grabbed the ball, dribbled, and dunked. I offered only abbreviated congratulations. Then I turned to the athletic director and pointedly told him to raise the basket back up to where it belonged. Impatient to grow taller, Jonathan had lowered the goal.

"Raise the basket, Jonathan," I said. "And try again."

He did. And he didn't make it. But he kept trying—and, in time, he made it.

Men, God has a standard. He has a goal. His kingdom is that goal. Yet what so many have done is lowered His standard only to then congratulate themselves for being able to dunk the ball. The results of this lowered standard, though, affect so many more than just the man on the court. A lowered standard affects us all. It shows up in our country. In our culture. In the economics of our world. It doesn't take much more than a cursory glance around our homes, churches, communities, and globe to uncover that men—not all, but many— have missed the goal to live as a kingdom man.

> *A lowered standard affects us all. It shows up in our country. In our culture.*

The impact of a lowered standard leaves its scars no matter what race, income bracket, or community a person is in. The outcomes may be different depending on the location, but they are just as devastating. Promiscuity, emptiness, depression, chronic irresponsibility, family breakup, misuse of finances, divorce, violence, chemical addiction, overeating, indulgence, bankruptcy, low self-esteem, and general aimlessness plague our society as a direct result of the abuse or neglect of biblical manhood.

The deterioration of societies both nearby and around the world has reached an all-time high, while the clarion call for men to come forth to stand for biblical manhood has never rung louder. Our world is on a disparaging path of self-destructive behavior.

That must change.

Yet that change will not occur unless men will raise the standard to where God had originally placed it. This book is about raising that standard and defining manhood as God intended it to be. It's about discovering what it means to be a kingdom man.

PART I

THE FORMATION OF A KINGDOM MAN

A kingdom man is a man who visibly demonstrates
the comprehensive rule of God underneath the Lordship
of Jesus Christ in every area of his life.

1

THE CRY FOR
A KINGDOM MAN

A kingdom man is the kind of man that when his feet hit the floor each morning the devil says, "Oh crap, he's up!"

When a kingdom man steps out his door each day, heaven, earth, and hell take notice. When he protects the woman under his care, she can do little to resist him. His children look to him with confidence. Other men look to him as someone to emulate. His church calls on him for strength and leadership. He is a preserver of culture and a champion of society to keep out evil and usher in good. A kingdom man understands that God never said a godly life would be easy; He just said it would be worth it.

Like a football player erupting from the tunnel at the start of a game, so starts a kingdom man each day. Not only does he take to the field in an explosion of fire, but he also dominates all opposition that rises against him. A kingdom man zeros in on one purpose and one purpose only—advancing the kingdom for the betterment of those within it, which glorifies the King. And he will pursue this at whatever personal cost.

As a chaplain for the Dallas Cowboys both now and during the height of the Tom Landry years, I've been to my share of NFL games. I also played football every evening and weekend from just about the time I was crawling until a leg injury requiring surgery ended my game. Yet no matter how many games I have gone to or played in, I have never heard a player complain that the opponents were too tough or that the goal was too difficult to obtain.

Anyone who has ever played or followed football knows that victory does not come just because you want it. Victory is earned only through sweat, guts, and blood. When nearly four quarters of a game have sucked the air from the heaving lungs of the linemen, battered the bodies of those carrying or chasing after the ball, and tortured the minds and muscles of everyone involved—a win often comes through nothing more than sheer determination. It comes to those who know that exhaustion is simply a word. And that *purpose* is far greater than *pain*.

The Third Team

Football is a man's sport. No doubt about it. It is the closest thing to an organized gladiator battle in our nation. In it, passion, strength, and power fuse with precision and skill as two teams face off in an epic display of both force and will. Yet unlike most battles and unlike most wars, a third team is in this conflict. Three teams take to the field.

In fact, this third team is intricately involved within every aspect of the fight that leads to the declaration of a victor.

Maybe you have never noticed that three teams are on the football field. But I guarantee that you would have noticed if the third team hadn't shown up. Because without this third team, there would be chaos on the field. There would be confusion in the face-off. In fact, there would be no way to play football as we know it.

> *Maybe you have never noticed that three teams are on the football field.*

This is because the third team is the team of officials.

The officials are unique in that their ultimate commitment is not to the teams on the field, nor do they align themselves with any of the other agendas. The officials' obligations do not lie with those who are in the battle, nor even with those watching it take place. Their commitment, as well as their allegiance, belongs to an entirely different kingdom called the NFL office. This kingdom supersedes, overrules, and sits above all others.

From the League office, the officials have been given a book. They have their own book with the governances, guidelines, rules, and regulations by which they are to manage the events on the field. While both teams are constantly pulling at the officials to choose a side, call penalties, or endorse plays, the team of officials must, in spite of personal preferences or emotions, rule according to its kingdom's book. Every decision made by every person on this third team must comply with the rulebook they have. It is their obligation to follow this book that has come directly from the commissioner—who has delegated authority to them.

If at any time an official makes a decision that sides with a team or a particular player—because of pressure from the fans, influence of players or coaching staff, or simply personal preferences—and that does not abide by the book, that official will have immediately lost the support and authority of not only the League office, but also of the commissioner. If the viewpoint of an official ever overrules the viewpoint of the book, superseding the kingdom to which the official is ultimately obligated, the official will no longer rule at all. This is because the NFL headquarters at 345 Park Avenue, New York, New York, will stand by an official only if that official stands by the book. Once an official leaves the book, he has just demoted himself to the status of a fan and become illegitimate in terms of his previously held authority.

Making the Call

Men, you are in a battle. You are in a war. The stakes of this war and its casualties are higher than a checkmark in the win or loss column. Lives will be lost. Eternities will be shaped. Destinies will either be discovered or dismissed. Dreams will be attained or relinquished.

Jesus has not asked you to be a fan. He has plenty of fans already. Every Sunday morning at 11:00 AM, His fan base shows up in full force. They show up in stadiums, often filled to capacity, all around the world. Within these stadiums, there is great emotion, great singing, preaching, excitement, cheers of adulation, recognition, and statements of affirmation. But Jesus is not interested in just having fans. No fan ever set the stage for a battle to be won. Jesus wants men who will carry out His agenda, governance, and guidelines in a world in crisis.

Jesus wants men who will rule well.

This kingdom of men has been intentionally placed in a location called Earth, yet these men receive their instructions from the League office in heaven. This group of men is neither swayed by what the majority says, nor by what the most popular thought at the moment might be, nor even by their own personal preferences. Rather, these men are governed by the kingdom to which they belong. Men who make their calls according to the Book under the authority of their Commissioner, the Lord Jesus Christ, so that chaos will not ensue in this war called life.

Jesus has not asked you to be a fan. He has plenty of fans already.

Keep in mind, that to rule something does not refer to domination or illegitimate control. Humankind's misuse of the term *rule* through dictatorships and abusive relationships has distorted the legitimate call on man to rule under God's sovereign rule and according to His principles.

In any game, as you might imagine, if the team of officials does not rule correctly, there is a loud cry not only from the stands or the people watching on their televisions but also from the players and coaches. There is a cry in response to the chaos taking place on the field—a cry for the officials to rule well.

The Cry for a Kingdom Man

If you listen closely, you might be able to hear the cry for kingdom men to rule well too. You can hear it in the chaos in the culture causing a cry to rise up from the homes, schools, neighborhoods, communities, states, and from every shattered soul affected by the absence of kingdom men. Never has our nation, or our world, stood on the precipice of adversity in such dire need of men answering the cry to rule well.

Listen.

It is everywhere. It is loud. It is in the heartbeat of every child born or raised without a father, every woman's dream drowned by an irresponsible or neglectful man, every hope snuffed out by confusing circumstances, every lonely soul of a single woman searching for someone worthy to marry, and every sanctuary and community devoid of significant male contributions.

It is a cry for a kingdom man.

If the team of officials stood on the sidelines of a game and never said a word about what was happening on the field, no one would go to the players who are committing the infractions and ask them why they are breaking the rules. Fans would look for the officials and demand, "Where are you? Get out there and do something." Because without the third team on the field, all battles would be chaos after the coin toss, leading to a loss of motivation, interest, and order. As a kingdom man, you have been commissioned by heaven to rule on Earth while wearing a different kind of stripe. You have been cut from a different kind of cloth because you represent a different kind of kingdom in this battle.

You represent the King.

And as a representative of the King, your purpose is much higher than merely your own and impacts a sphere much wider than you may ever know.

As a kingdom man, there is more to you than you may have even realized.

The Kingdom Ruler

The Greek word used for *kingdom* in the New Testament is *basileia*,[1] which means authority and rule. A kingdom always includes three fundamental components: a ruler, a realm of subjects who fall under his rule, and the rules or governances. The kingdom of God is the authoritative execution of His comprehensive rule in all creation. The kingdom agenda is simply the visible demonstration of the comprehensive rule of God over every area of life.[2]

God's kingdom transcends time, space, politics, denominations, cultures, and the realms of society. It is both now and not yet (see Mark 1:15 and Matthew 16:28), close by and removed (see Luke 17:20–21 and Matthew 7:21). Governed by covenant systems, the kingdom's institutions include the family, church, and civil government. God has given the guidelines for the operation of all three, and negligence to adhere to these guidelines results in disorder and loss.

While each of the three fundamental components maintains separate responsibilities and dominion, all three are to work in conjunction with the others under divine rule based on an absolute standard of truth. When the components work this way, they bring order to a world of confusion and promote personal responsibility under God.

The primary component upon which all else rests in a kingdom is the authority of the ruler. Without that, there is anarchy resulting in mess. Knowing this is exactly why Satan's very first move in the garden was to subtly and deceitfully dethrone the ruler. Before we read about Satan approaching Eve in the garden, every Scripture reference to God in relation to Adam is made as LORD God. Anytime you read the word LORD (in all caps), it refers to the name Yahweh used for God. The special title Yahweh means master and absolute ruler[3] and is the name God used to reveal himself in His relationship with man. Prior to the name Yahweh, God had revealed himself as Creator, which is the name Elohim.

However, when Satan spoke to Eve about eating that which she should not, he did not refer to God as LORD God. Satan essentially stripped off the name LORD—removing master and absolute ruler—and instead said, "Indeed, has God said . . ." Thus Satan sought to reduce God's rulership over humankind by beginning with the subtle but effective twist of His name. In doing so, Satan kept the concept of religion while eliminating divine authority.

> *Satan sought to reduce God's rulership over humankind by beginning with the subtle but effective twist of His name.*

By removing LORD from the authoritative nature of the relationship between God and Adam and Eve and in bypassing Adam, Satan not only caused humankind to rebel, but he also took over the dominion that man was supposed to be exercising under God's authority. By eating the fruit in disobedience, Adam and Eve chose to change how they viewed their Creator from LORD God to God, resulting in the loss of their intimate fellowship with Him and each other, as well as the power of the dominion that flows from the ultimate Ruler.

Even though Eve ate the fruit first, God went looking for Adam. It had been Adam whom God had revealed himself to as LORD God in the context of giving Adam divine instruction. As a result, when the title of master and absolute ruler was removed, Adam was ultimately held responsible.

Ever since then a continual battle has existed over who will rule humankind. This is because Adam's importance wasn't simply that he was the first man God made. Rather, Adam was to be the prototype that all men were to seek to become.

Therefore, when men make decisions based on their own thoughts, beliefs, or values—like Adam—rather than based on what God has to say as Ruler, then men are choosing to rule themselves as Adam did. They are choosing to call the King *God* without recognizing His authority by removing His rightful name of LORD God or Lord God, also found in Scripture referring to *'adown*[4] (master)— the verbal parallel to *Yahweh*. Essentially, they—like Adam—are seeking to dethrone their own Creator while still recognizing His existence.

It is religion without the ruler relationship of *Yahweh*.

There are two answers to every question—God's answer and everyone else's. When they contradict, everyone else is wrong. Removing master and absolute ruler from God's relationship with man essentially places God's answer on the same level as everyone else's. Adam's sin was allowing his wife's human viewpoint, which had been initiated by Satan, to override the revealed will and Word of God. Adam allowed a person close to him to overrule God.

Men, only by putting LORD back into the equation will you experience the dominion and authority you were created to have.

God's Authority

God told the Israelites, as described in Exodus 34:23, that three times a year all of their males were to appear together before Him to receive instructions from Him. Yet when God told them to appear, He specifically called them out before the "Lord GOD, the God of Israel." He called them to submit themselves to His complete authority.

If the men submitted, they were told that they, and those connected to them, would receive God's covering, protection, and provision. But they would receive this only if they positioned themselves under His absolute rule. So essential was this element of rulership that God used three of His names as a reminder. The Israelites were told to appear before the

- Lord (*'adown*)
- GOD (*Jehova*)[5]
- God of Israel (*'Elohim*)[6]

God was in charge, to the third power. In using three different names for himself, God emphasized His supreme authority over the men of the nation and their accountability to Him.

The same principle of God's rulership that applied to the Israelites is no different than God's rulership today. He is God—*Lord, GOD, God of Israel,* master, supreme God, ruler, and judge. A kingdom man, therefore, is *one who visibly demonstrates the comprehensive rule of God underneath the Lordship of Jesus Christ in every area of his life.* Rather than Adam being the prototype for man, now Jesus Christ—as the last Adam (1 Corinthians 15:45)—is the prototype for a kingdom man.

> *The same principle of God's rulership that applied to the Israelites is no different than God's rulership today.*

A kingdom man is a man who rules according to God's rule.

Just as a referee in an NFL game is able to rule only according to the rulebook, a kingdom man is released to rule when he makes his decisions and orders his world according to God's rule.

When a kingdom man functions according to the principles and precepts of the kingdom, there will be order, authority, and provision. Yet when he doesn't, he opens himself up, and those connected to him, to a life of chaos.

The Miracle on the Hudson

The Hudson River runs through New York City—at one point actually separating Manhattan from the New Jersey border. The Hudson swells with both history and heritage. It is also one of the most scenic rivers in the United States, earning it the nickname of "America's Rhine."

Two occurrences on the Hudson grabbed my attention recently because each reveals what happens when a man rules, or does not rule, his realm well.

The first happened in 2009 during the icy cold month of January when birds flew straight into the engines of US Airways Flight 1549 immediately after the plane's takeoff, simultaneously shutting down both engines.

With only minutes until what seemed like an inevitable disaster, the pilot contacted the air control tower to seek clearance for rerouting and an emergency landing. He was told to return to the LaGuardia Airport.

At that point the captain, Chesley B. Sullenberger III, had to make a decision. The airport wasn't close enough for landing, so Sullenberger's only option was to ditch the plane in the Hudson. Yet landing a wide-bodied commercial plane on water without accruing fatalities was unlikely. Sullenberger, a veteran pilot of four decades, was acutely aware that the odds were not in favor of his surviving. Having served as a flight instructor, accident investigator, and flight crew instructor, Sullenberger didn't have to dig too deep in his mind to ascertain what the outcome could be.

Yet with two engines out and nowhere else for the plane to go, Sullenberger took charge of the realm for which he was responsible. Against the backdrop of passengers crying out for someone to bring order to the chaos, Sullenberger made a few quick adjustments, kept the plane just high enough to fly over the George Washington Bridge, and did what few pilots have ever attempted to do—he ditched the plane in the river. Ninety seconds before landing, he addressed the frantic cries of the passengers, stating calmly, "Brace for impact."

What happened next was nothing short of a perfect textbook ditching. In order for a plane not to break up on water impact, it has to land at precisely the correct speed as well as at precisely the correct level. Sullenberger gently pulled up on the nose of the plane, leveled the wings, and adjusted the speed simultaneously upon hitting the water to prevent the plane from breaking into a thousand pieces. And he did this with a jarring, violently vibrating 80-ton piece of metal.

While the icy cold water began to pour inside the plane after landing, passengers and crew rushed to the emergency exits as Captain Sullenberger directed the evacuation. Once the last person was off of the airplane, Sullenberger made two more passes through the length of the plane to be certain that everyone had gotten off safely. With water midway up the interior, Sullenberger was the final person to disembark Flight 1549.

All souls on board survived.

The years Sullenberger exercised responsibility as an Air Force pilot, an accident investigator, an airline safety consultant and safety manager—let alone more than 19,000 hours logged of uneventful flight time—had prepared him with the necessary skills and mind-set to rule the realm of his plane well, rather than his plane ruling him.

As a result, Sullenberger not only prevented his own teenage daughters from becoming orphans and his wife from becoming a widow, but he also preserved the lives and legacies of 155 people, the youngest of which was a nine-month-old boy. New York Governor David Paterson called the incident the "Miracle on the Hudson."[7]

Tragedy on the Hudson

Something other than a miracle happened on the Hudson two years later. It is a true yet tragic story about a twenty-five-year-old woman. Her story, while her own, reflects the countless stories of others just like her—abandoned and broken by the neglect or mistreatment of the man, or men, in her life.

At the age of fifteen, she had her first child. Within a few more years, she added three more children by a different man—giving each of the next three children their father's last name, Pierre, as their middle name. It was a heritage that shouldn't have been passed on.

The children's father didn't marry their mother. He had been arrested for not paying child support for months on end. Another time he was arrested when their two-year-old son, having been left in his custody at his apartment completely alone, wandered out on a frigid February night. Police eventually found the toddler at 1:15 AM crying near a busy street, partially dressed in wet clothing.

Neighbors and family say that the mom loved her children. They always looked well cared-for, groomed, and appeared well-behaved. Mom was taking classes at the local community college and working—probably trying to better her life.

But on a cold April 2011 day, she posted an apology on Facebook, called her mother, grandmother, and father to say good-bye, loaded up all four kids in her van, and drove straight into the freezing waters of the Hudson.

As the van began to sink, her ten-year-old struggled to open the locked doors or roll down a window while the younger kids cried out in fear. He was able to squeeze himself out of a window before the van went under. He later told police that his mom had gathered all of the kids around her, held them, and said, "If I am going to die, you are going to die with me."

Neighbors say that the father of the three younger children had shown up at her house just an hour before she drove her children to their deaths. He pounded on her apartment door screaming threats for over thirty minutes. This wasn't the first altercation the couple had had.

No ones knows what ultimately drove her to take drastic measures. But less than an hour after the father had left, the young mother and three of her four children were dead in the Hudson River. Her children's final tears undoubtedly cried out in hopes of someone to stop the chaos of their world. No one did.[8]

Some people may blame this young mother for her actions. And her actions were horrific. But a shared blame for a woman who takes her own life and her children's directly following a volatile situation from the father of her children also belongs to the man.

Her last words, "If I am going to die, you are going to die with me," is a revealing statement because it reflects the power of a man's impact, for good or for bad. Innocent children may suffer a death of their destiny, hopes, dreams, esteem, futures, and possibly even their lives when a man's failure to rule well snuffs out the life of their mother—whether that be a literal, emotional, or spiritual death.

One hundred fifty-five people survived a crash landing on the Hudson because one man operated with responsibility in his realm. Four people died in the icy grip of the same river because one man—or perhaps several—did not.

Which Way Will You Go?

An interesting fact about the Hudson River that I didn't mention earlier is that it is one of only a few rivers that runs in two directions. While tides from the Atlantic move the river northward, the origin of the river at Lake Tear of the Clouds also moves the currents southward. Before being named the Hudson River, it was called by local American Indian tribes *Muhheakantuck*, which means the river that flows two ways.

Just as the Hudson has been hailed as a place of life—the miracle on the Hudson—and a place of death—"You are going to die with me"—life has a way of also flowing both ways. Yet a lot of that depends on you. A lot of that depends on whether you are a kingdom man who responsibly rules with consistency and wisdom according to the guidelines and governances set forth in God's Word. Or whether you are a man of this world, leaving those under your influence vulnerable not only to what life brings their way but also vulnerable to themselves as a result of the chaos that you have either made or allowed.

If you are a man, like it or not, you are a leader by position. It could be that you are a horrible one by practice, but by position, you have been called to lead. That is what the Adam prototype entailed. God created Adam before Eve because he was to be responsible to both rule and lead. Adam was given his calling to cultivate and guard the garden before Eve was even created. And, as a result, it was Adam whom God sought when both Adam and Eve had disobeyed Him.

This is because Adam was ultimately responsible.

As a man, you are ultimately responsible for those within your domain.

> *God created Adam before Eve because he was to be responsible to both rule and lead.*

Men, how you lead will play a large part in either the life or death experienced within your realm. You can either lead those in your care to a place of safety, or you can drive those in your care to a place of chaos. But to rule well is not a call that you make one day and then forget about. Ruling well is a lifelong skill forged through faithfulness and dedication. Sullenberger didn't land his plane on the water simply because he thought it would be an awesome thing to do. In order to be the hero that day, he had to show up day in and day out, year in and year out, decade in and decade out, intentionally and consistently applying himself to ruling his realm well.

Captain Sullenberger's commitment to meet the expectations of those he serves in the aviation industry ought to inspire each of us to an even greater level of dedication in fulfilling that which the King of the universe has called us to do.

The King has given you a rulebook by which you are to govern—by which you are to rule, lead, make decisions, direct, guide, and align your life choices. This rulebook is His Word. When you lead according to what He says in His Word, He will back you with the authority you need to carry it out. Yet when you don't, you are on your own. Men, many tomorrows will be determined by how well you rule today.

When you lead according to His principles and His kingdom agenda, you free others around you to be what they were created to be as well. Yet when you don't, you invite a world of chaos, disorder, and destruction not only into your own life, but also into the lives of those within your influence.

As a kingdom man, you are on the third team sent here to bring heaven's rule into a world in need. But this isn't a game. This is a real battle. This is a war. A spiritual war. You may not be able to see your enemy directly, but his presence is revealed all around you.

When your feet hit the floor each morning, do you make your enemy the devil, say, "Oh crap, he's up"?

When you step out your door each day, do heaven, earth, and hell take notice? When you protect the woman under your care, can she do little to resist you? Do your children look to you with confidence? Do other men look to you as someone to emulate? Does your church call on you for strength and leadership? Are you a preserver of culture and a champion of society, one who keeps out evil and ushers in good? Are you a man who is fulfilling your destiny and able to satisfy the woman in your life?

More than all of that, though, when God searches for a man to advance His kingdom, does He call your name?

2

THE CONCEPT OF A KINGDOM MAN

As a pastor, I have seen my fair share of casualties resulting from an absence of kingdom men. Just within the last few weeks, I have counseled ten couples in a last-ditch effort to save what they feel they have already lost. Having offered marital counseling for over thirty-five years, I've observed that the problem usually boils down to one thing: one or both parties are out of alignment. So few men understand what it means to be in alignment under God, and yet most will fiercely require their wife to align under them.

I don't often have to look much farther than the first pew to recognize casualties in the congregation that have occurred as a result of either the misuse, abuse, neglect, or confusion of kingdom manhood. What I see and hear while counseling doesn't surprise me as much as the frequency with which I encounter it these days. It is as if we have fallen into an abyss of manlessness.

Not only do I see the results of this abyss in the church, but I witness casualties outside of the church as well. For example, I witness these casualties when I go to preach at a local prison.

What strikes me as I walk through the security checkpoints and experience the isolation that inevitably comes with being inside a prison facility is how each of these prisoners had, at one point, been free. Not only that, but each of them also had, at one point, been a child and free—running barefoot, playing games, or falling asleep with dreams of slaying dragons and claiming possibilities. If we were to look at their family histories, however, most of them not only lacked a man to protect and guide them, but also the prisoners had suffered under the negative impact of one man or many. As a result, each of the prisoners now slept in a cold cell covered by only a thin blanket of abandonment, shame, insecurity, and regret.

I mentioned these prisoners when I spoke at an event on the church's role in community restoration in Plano, Texas. Ironically, this event was held in a building called the Hope Center. Yet the statistics of fatherlessness surrounding the inmates left little room for hope of much changing in the next generation unless men en masse begin to answer the call to be kingdom men. Roughly 70 percent of all prisoners come from fatherless homes.[1] Approximately 80 percent of all rapists with anger problems come from fatherless homes.[2] The statistics on fatherlessness outside of the prison population are just as alarming. Seventy-one percent of all high school dropouts come from fatherless homes; 63 percent of all teen suicides occur in homes where the father was either abusive or absent.[3] In suburbia, many fathers have gone "missing" either through divorce, neglect, or overindulgence. Many fathers put their careers over their families, or they love the golf course more than they love their kids.

In suburbia, many fathers have gone "missing" either through divorce, neglect, or overindulgence.

Fatherlessness, whether it comes through outright abandonment or through more subtle forms of abandonment, leaves similar scars on those affected by it. Virtually every adult social pathology has been linked to either fatherless homes or homes with a father and/or husband who was absent, abusive, or neglectful.[4]

To many of us living a comfortable life outside of these statistical realities, those numbers may seem impersonal and easy to ignore, but the effects of those statistics impact us all. On average, taxpayers spend more than $8 billion annually on high school dropouts for public assistance programs such as food stamps, according to a May 2010 report by CBS News.[5] High school dropouts also earn an average of $260,000 less in their lifetime than graduates—giving our nation a cumulative loss of over $300 billion annually in earned taxable revenue.[6] Teen pregnancies cost American taxpayers an average of $10 billion annually in public assistance, lost revenue, and increased health care costs.[7] And with the prison population having nearly tripled from 1987 to 2007 to the highest per capita rate in the world,[8] we now spend over $52 billion a year on prisons.[9]

Society's problems are not just society's problems. They are the church's problems. They are our problems. The consequences of society's problems reach us all and have caused our nation to now stand on the brink of economic collapse.

The inmates at the prison I visit came from different cultures, backgrounds, generations, and experiences. They had committed different crimes. But one thing that most shared was that they had either come from a fatherless home or a home where the father was absent, neglectful, or abusive.

When I looked into their eyes—both the men and the women—I didn't see statistics. I didn't see numbers on a page. I saw real pain, real emptiness, real longing, real anger, real loss, and real need. I wish you could have seen it too because statistics can never tell the story of a soul.

Looking at the Casualties

But I don't need to take you to the prison with me next time to show you what happens to people when a man fails to live as a kingdom man. It is possible that you need to look only at your own siblings, wife, or children. I hope not, but it's possible. Or maybe you need to look only at your neighbor's child or children or the youth in your church. The brokenness of homes. The decay of the family. The headlines in the news. The breakdown of our nation.

To say that men have lost their identity is an understatement. Casualties abound of men not fulfilling their God-given role to provide leadership and mirror God's character and management. In fact, I could have been one of those casualties myself. When I was ten, all I had ever known up until that point was chaos in my home. I was the oldest of four children, and the atmosphere was volatile for all of us. My father and mother were in constant conflict, making divorce seem like the only possible outcome. But what my dad modeled for me the year that I turned ten forever changed my life. That was the year my dad turned to Jesus. But my dad didn't just accept God's salvation; he immediately became fired up about God and the Bible. He became an instant evangelist, consumed with God's Word.

My mom didn't like my dad as a sinner, and she liked him even less as a saint.

After my dad became a Christian, my mom did everything she could to make his life difficult. My dad couldn't even read his Bible until after my mom went to sleep because she would make his life so miserable when he did. But my dad was committed to aligning himself under God, so my father did everything he could to show love to my mom in spite of how she treated him.

Rather than divorce her, he loved her unconditionally. Day after day and month after month, my mom tried anything and everything to knock my dad's focus off of God and to make him stop loving her. But nothing worked. My dad was calm, consistent, and caring.

Around midnight one night, my mom came down the stairs with tears in her eyes. My dad was reading his Bible. When he saw her tears, he asked her what was wrong. She told him that she could not understand how the more she rejected him, was unkind to him, and tried to prove that believing in God was wrong, the more kind he was to her and the more he invested in the Word.

> *My father did everything he could to show love to my mom in spite of how she treated him.*

"I want what you have," she said, "because it must be real."

They both instantly got down on their knees, and my dad led my mom to Christ. After that, he led all of us kids to Christ and daily modeled for us the value of making God and His Word the central focus in all that we did.

If my dad had not exhibited the courage to be dedicated to God and to his family even in spite of harsh opposition, my own home would have become a statistic. I would have ended up as a casualty. Yet not only would I have ended up as a casualty, but my own children may have ended up as casualties too.

The impact a father has on a home, the impact a husband has on a marriage, and the impact a man has on a church or community cannot be emphasized enough. My father's impact dramatically altered the trajectory of my life and, as a result, has impacted more people than he will ever know this side of heaven.

Conversely, the absence of kingdom men has not only left many of our families weakened and vulnerable to attack but has also ushered our nation into one of the most delicate positions economically, socially, and spiritually that we have ever been.

Adam, Where You At?

The question on the floor as we begin our journey into this area of becoming a kingdom man is "How did we end up here in the first place?" How did we—a nation founded on principles of communal and personal spiritual responsibility— end up drowning in a sea of so many irresponsible men? The answer to that question isn't as complex as you might imagine. In fact, it all has to do with the kingdom's Book. Somewhere along the line, we have forgotten to check with the Book by which we are to rule.

Not long ago my daughter-in-law Kanika appeared on the television game show *Wheel of Fortune*. Spinning the wheel and solving the puzzles was no problem for Kanika. At the end of the show, she brought home a large prize—much to the pride of her husband, Jonathan. Yet regardless of how well Kanika had done in the game, she wasn't able to win the final round.

When Kanika gave the letters that she hoped would appear in the final word puzzle, only one letter showed up, leaving most of the puzzle blank. Even the host admitted that this one was a challenge. Kanika just didn't have enough letters to form a word in only ten seconds.

Kanika's situation resembles the contemporary setting of many men's situations today. We have a little bit of the definition of manhood here or a little bit over there, but since we are not defining manhood by the complete Word of God—the Book—we are staring at a definition with missing letters and missing words. We are trying to fill in those letters with our own words, our own thoughts, and our own understanding. But at the end of the day, the buzzer sounds and we wind up empty-handed.

We can't expect to understand or live out God's definition of manhood without applying all of the content of His Word. An official who referees a game by only a portion of the rulebook would be fired in an instant. Yet, for some reason, we as men have failed to realize that we must live by the complete Word of God. Whenever the Word of God is distorted, limited, or reduced in its overarching rule in a man's life, casualties will abound. Just as they do today. Just as they did in the garden thousands of years ago. Just as they did with Adam.

Any discussion on the role, purpose, and leadership of a man must begin with Adam. The theology of Adam isn't merely an Old Testament concept. The theology of man's responsibility based on the order of creation and that which God assigned him is carried through the New Testament and even into the church age (see 1 Timothy 2:12-14; 3:1; 1 Corinthians 11:3). The reason we are not able to find men manning their post today is the same reason God walked through the garden so long ago saying, "Adam, where are you?" Or as we say it where I come from, "Adam, where you at?"

The reason Adam could not be found in the garden that day is the same thing that causes so many single women difficulty in locating a kingdom man today. And the same reason why so many married women are frustrated with the men that they've got. This is also the same reason why pastors and church leaders are finding it difficult to garrison men to their post. This reason is that men have misunderstood their role to rule and to lead as kingdom men.

> *The biblical concept of dominion, or rule, is neither a dictatorship nor a posture of domination.*

Keep in mind that I have intentionally chosen to use the often inflammatory word *rule* in relationship to a man's destiny on Earth because, despite the bad press the word has been given by the world, a man's rule—when carried out under the overarching rule of God—is a liberating leadership not only for him, but also for those around him. The biblical concept of dominion, or rule, is neither a dictatorship nor a posture of domination, but rather it entails exercising legitimate authority under the lordship of Jesus Christ. Legitimate authority entails all that God provides for and permits a man to do, but not all that a man wishes to do.

Men have misunderstood their right to rule not only because of the stigma created by those who have done it poorly, but also because we, in the body of Christ, have too frequently ignored the teachings on God's kingdom. As a result, we have failed to understand kingdom theology and kingdom rule. While Christ walked this planet, He often spoke of God's rule through His kingdom. In fact, Jesus mentioned the *church*, or the Greek *ekklesia*, only three times as recorded in His earthly ministry, and all three times are in the kingdom-minded gospel of Matthew.[10] However, the Greek word for kingdom, *basileia*—meaning rule or authority—is mentioned 162 times in the New Testament.[11]

My concern is that Christian leaders have leveraged our men to build church buildings and run church programs, but we have failed to disciple them in what it means to be about the kingdom. Nothing is wrong with church buildings—as long as those within it aim to use the available resources strategically to advance God's kingdom.

God's kingdom consists of His comprehensive governance in all creation. His agenda is to advance His kingdom and, in so doing, to reveal His glory. God's subjects have been put here on Earth to carry out His agenda. Therefore, a kingdom man may be defined as *a man who positions himself and operates according to the comprehensive rule of God over every area of his life.* And every area of life should feel the impact of a kingdom man's presence.

You Are Responsible

One of the critical elements to advance God's kingdom is understanding that, as a man, you are responsible for that which falls within the realm of influence that God has given you: your family, ministry, career, resources, community, or other areas of personal influence. A man who foregoes responsibility in the chaos or confusion of his realm, even if it is his direct doing, has thus prevented himself from remedying it. Not only does he lack God's power to advance, but he has also disqualified himself from even fixing what has been broken.

I pastor a well-established church with over 200 employees. Most of the time, the church runs smoothly and I am not involved in the day-to-day logistics. Yet occasionally I will get a phone call from someone in the congregation who sounds upset and tells me something that he or she does not like.

I'll never forget the time a woman called to tell me that she had phoned the church five times the day before and could not get through to the receptionist any of those times. Every time this particular woman had called the church, the receptionist had been unable to answer, so the woman's call had gone to voice mail.

Now, when I get a call like that, I have to stop myself from telling the caller on the other end of the line the parable of the persistent widow and encourage her to try a sixth time. Seriously, though, my normal reaction would be to ask her why she is giving her complaint to me and not to the receptionist. I am the senior pastor, after all, of a several-hundred staff-run church, Christian school, and outreach center. How am I supposed to know why the receptionist wasn't there at those precise moments? Maybe she was on other calls. No offense, but ask her.

Yet even though that is what I feel like saying, that is not what I actually say. Because, in all honesty, the caller is right. She has tracked down and contacted the correct person for her complaint.

As senior pastor, I may not be directly to blame for the issue regarding the missed phone calls, but my position makes me ultimately responsible. And when I do get a call or complaint, trust me, I seek to handle it immediately so it doesn't happen again. Why? Because I am ultimately responsible to see that it doesn't happen again.

The same complaint got brought to Adam. Not about a phone call, but about a piece of fruit. Even though it was Eve whom the serpent tempted to eat the fruit that had been forbidden in the garden of Eden (Genesis 3:1–6), it was Adam whom God went looking for. After all, Adam was responsible. We read in Genesis 3:9, "Then the LORD God called to the man, and said to him, 'Where are you?' " Notice, God reasserted His authority in His relationship with Adam by saying, "Then the LORD God called to the man . . ." Likewise, nowhere do we read that He said, "Adam and Eve, where are y'all?"

Irrespective of who did what first, the question is posed to Adam because Adam was accountable under God as the assigned representative to carry out, and to assure the carrying out of God's agenda. While Eve bore responsibility for her part, Adam was also held responsible because of his leadership position.

Adam had been placed in the garden both to cultivate and keep it (Genesis 2:15). To cultivate the land meant to make it productive and to develop its potential. Out of the productivity of the land, Adam would have what he needed to provide for those within his care. The Hebrew word used for *keep* was *shamar* and it meant to guard or have charge of.[12] At the time, Adam was to guard the garden from Satan, who is still the main threat to our lives and families today. Spiritual warfare was there at Adam's inception, as well as at our own. Yet because Satan doesn't typically show up in a red jumpsuit with bloodshot eyes and a pitchfork, we often miss the subtleties of his deception, although their ramifications are far reaching.

When lordship was removed from God's relationship with Adam, that led to sin and disobedience. This in turn caused misalignment between Adam and God, which resulted in decay, destruction, and death. Satan's removal of the concept of *LORD* is a major problem, as we saw earlier in Genesis 3, but it isn't the only problem. Likewise, the deception of Eve is a central problem in the same chapter.

But the greater problem was that Adam had nothing to say while both things happened. Genesis 3 introduces us to a long-standing problem among men: the silence of Adam.

Up until the serpent and the fruit, Adam had been doing a lot of talking. He hadn't been quiet at all. In fact, Adam had been naming things right and left. But when the serpent showed up, Adam had nothing to say to it or to the woman. Instead, he sat back while the two interacted.

I say that Adam allowed this interaction because, contrary to what many of us learned in Bible storybooks that portrayed images of the event, Eve was not alone in this conversation. Genesis 3:6 says, ". . . and she gave also to her husband *with her* . . ." The whole time the serpent was talking, Adam was there. Silent. Even when Eve turned to him and laid down a new agenda for their home, Adam didn't say a thing. He just ate.

> *Spiritual warfare was there at Adam's inception, as well as at our own.*

As a result of Adam's silent choice, God pronounced that the ground that he worked from then on would be cursed (see verses 17–19). What used to require little by way of sweat and physical effort would now demand toil and struggle from Adam because of the abdication of his role.

One of the reasons that so many of our children are living under the heaviness of struggle, or that so many of our families are living under the weight of turmoil, or that so many of our churches are operating under the cloud of confusion, or that our nation is scrambling to salvage its strength is because Adam had nothing to say. Adam is still hiding in many ways. And in so doing, Adam willingly relinquished his God-given right to leadership. First Corinthians 11:3 clearly delineates equality between men and women but outlines distinctions in roles and responsibilities.

The problem keeping many men in our culture from being kingdom men is that, either through silence or blame, they have relinquished their God-given right to rule, or lead. Adam did both, and today many men do the same. In doing so, they have given up their opportunity to approach the Christian life as a challenge and a quest to conquer and have instead settled to live as responders.

Men, you do have an enemy to conquer. You have a legion of his minions coming at you and at those you love every day in a head-to-head competition to see who will walk away with the glory—either Satan or God.

One of the greatest failures, I believe, of the American church has been that we have not equipped men to fully understand, realize, and implement their divine destiny of biblical manhood. We have stripped them of their manhood while attempting to redefine it with things such as church attendance in churches primarily geared toward women (from the decorations on the walls to the music to the short-lived and often less effective mission trips, and to the service on numerous committees). While each of those things is important, and good, without a common vision on a common goal against a common enemy—we often wind up simply busier than deliberately strategic.

It is the rare man who finds himself satisfied with being *busy* more than accomplishing the greatest possibilities through maximizing the resources at his disposal. Yet by dangling the carrot of *busy*, often untied to intentional and long-term approaches for conquering the enemy and advancing the kingdom, we have left the door wide open to having manhood defined by what seems to be more tantalizing concepts such as Wall Street, fast cars, faster women, and how high a man can climb up the corporate ladder. Not only is Adam silent in many ways today, but the church has become silent too. By dissuading, or at least downplaying, the presence of the drive in men to conquer and compete within much of formalized Western Christianity, we have essentially ripped out a man's lungs and then blamed him for not breathing.

A number of things happen to a man when he can no longer breathe. One of these is that he becomes passive. He lives in the world of indecision, allowing everyone around him to dictate to him what to do, how to think, or what to value. And then he blames everyone else when things go wrong. Any man who blames his wife for the chaos in his home without simultaneously accepting responsibility for addressing it is publicly declaring his lack of biblical manhood. I have counseled enough men to know that although they may appear satisfied on the outside, many are feeling smothered and gasping within because they do not know how to be a man.

Another thing that happens to a man when he can no longer breathe is that he will try to live vicariously through others. This shows up in the enormous number of sports fanatics we have in our country. I didn't say sports fans—but fanatics. It is men who will wear another man's jersey with another man's name and number on the back of it. Regularly. Any man who has to wear another man's name on the back of his shirt may need to ask himself how he views his own manhood.

Or it is men who will live vicariously through characters in action films or television shows packed full of barely clothed women, adventure, and intrigue. It is men who don't man up in their own bedroom by caring for the woman they are with so she freely responds and engages with him, but, instead, chooses to seek secondhand gratification through pornography. Pornography use is one of the greatest indicators that a man has lost touch with his own manhood since he has to piggyback on the intimacy of others.

One of the most damaging things to the people around a man who has either lost his ability to breathe or is too afraid to try is that he becomes controlling, dominating, and either emotionally or physically abusive to someone weaker than himself. This typically shows up in the home between the husband and the wife. Although he may seem friendly, cooperative, and respectful at work, this man criticizes

> *Pornography use is one of the greatest indicators that a man has lost touch with his own manhood.*

his wife, withholds affection, controls her spending and social life, and limits her personal and professional development so she remains in a constant state of forced dependency on him. He does this because he does not know how to feel or exercise legitimate power, so he seeks to dominate someone weaker than himself.

Legitimate power is power under the control and authority within the clearly defined boundaries of God. It is power surrendered to God's rules—first and foremost His primary rules to live in a way that reflects and manifests your love for Him and your love for others.

Men were created to breathe. Yet when society is the only one offering the gateway for breath, and when the gateway it offers is an illegitimate expression of manhood, the church has done a disservice to men. Because no greater legitimate authority for rule exists apart from God. And when men do not understand that they have been uniquely designed to lead within the domain in which they have been placed, they are left with a confusing definition of manhood that will wind up hurting not only themselves but also those around them.

I've Got It

There is nothing I love more about my life than being a man. I love my wife. I love my family. I love my calling (and, like I said earlier, I love football). But all of that rests on the fulfillment of a greater reality—of being a man. Sometimes when I wake up in the morning, before my feet even hit the floor, I say, "Evans, it is great to be a man." The whole day looms ahead begging to be explored, experienced, and conquered.

Something is inherent in the DNA of manhood that urges men to rise to the occasion, solve the equation, protect, defend, defeat, and restore. Life's challenges taunt us to defy them. Responsibilities call us to fulfill them.

I love being a man.

But within that love lies an even greater passion to equip and empower other men to realize the full expression of their manhood within the prevailing intricacies of the kingdom of God. If you are a man, you ought to love being a man. More than that, you ought to love being a kingdom man. To be a kingdom man is every man's destiny. And every woman dreams of being with one. Because when a kingdom man rules his realm well, everyone benefits.

Everyone can rest well.

In the Evans home, we have a sign. I can't remember exactly when I started doing it, but when a problem comes up or a legitimate issue gives rise to worry or concern, I will sometimes raise three fingers. That's all. When I raise three fingers, and without having to say a word, I can immediately see the tension leave my wife's face or whomever it is I am talking to. It goes away because those three fingers remind them of three words: *I've got it.*

I've got it.

When I say *I've got it* that means that whomever I'm saying it to doesn't have to carry it, worry about it, or try to figure it out. I'll take responsibility for it. And if it is something that I cannot solve, I will provide the comfort, stability, and empathy that are necessary to get through it. It doesn't mean that I literally and tangibly do everything. It means that I see to it that everything is done.

As a man, when you have demonstrated to a woman, children, or people within your sphere of influence that you are dependable, responsible, and that you take ownership to fix, solve, or simply carry the burden of that which cannot be solved, you have freed them to rest. You have freed them to relax because they know that they can trust the man who has proven to them through past actions that he's got it. As a kingdom man, those around you need to know that *you've got it.*

It is no different than what God does for us when He tells us not to worry. Essentially, God says,

"Fear not, *I've got it.*"
"Don't worry, *I've got it.*"
"Be still, *I've got it.*"

God's covering over us as His sons is a model of how we as men are to cover those under us. To cover someone or to be someone's covering simply means that you provide the protection and provision they need, as well as an environment for nurturing and fostering emotional, spiritual, and physical health. Men, when God's got it and you are leading and living according to His principles and under His governance, your faith in Him comes through in how you relate to those around you. Essentially, *you've got it* because you are putting your trust in and functioning according to the truth that *God's got it.*

> *God's covering over us as His sons is a model of how we as men are to cover those under us.*

One of the most visual reflections I have of this covering is a bronze statue of a male eagle with his wings spread out covering the mother eagle and their eaglets. The statue sits in a prominent location in my office at the church to serve as a reminder of my role over those within my realm. Like the eagle protecting those under his care, God doesn't sit down on the couch and turn on the television when someone needs Him. Neither does He run off to work as a get-away excuse. Rather, He takes responsibility to comfort those within a crisis or correct the situation.

You've Got It

Your destiny as a kingdom man means fulfilling your divinely designed reason for being to glorify God by advancing His kingdom. Fused within every kingdom man's urge to conquer ought to be an equally strong conviction to cover. That covering includes taking responsibility for that which God has placed in your care. You can take this responsibility, men, even if you don't feel like you have the skills, wisdom, or ability to handle it, if you will simply align yourself under God because *He's got it*. It is all a matter of alignment.

To be aligned under God is to consistently make your decisions, whether personal or professional, in line with God's Word. This means intentionally going to the Scriptures and often to a person acquainted with the Scriptures on a specific matter that you are dealing with. For example, if you are seeking to resolve a financial issue or to establish sound financial principles and stewardship in your life, you look up everything that you can find in God's Word on it and start applying it to your life.

When I was a young married man just starting a church, finishing up my doctorate, and beginning the process of financially planning for our future, I read everything that I could in Scripture about how to handle the money God had given to us. Then, to make sure that I aligned myself with God's Word, I sought out those who were knowledgeable about finances and God's wisdom on the topic. Larry Burkett agreed to meet with me to guide me on how to handle the very little money that we had as a family in order to avoid going into debt while juggling the expense of seminary coupled with the reduced income that comes with planting a church. That is a practical example of how to intentionally align yourself under God.

However, sometimes a situation will come up in my home or at the church that makes me think to myself, *There is no way I will be able to remedy this one. It is too deep, too messy, or too chaotic, and nothing in Scripture specifically addresses the details of the issue—other than to trust God, have faith, and honor Him.* But do you know what I do when that happens? I still hold up three fingers. And I hold them up as if I mean it—not because I am pretending to have it, but because, as a man under God, I have faith that God has it. That way those around me can rest because it is my way of communicating to them that they can let go of the burden because I've got it. And the reason that I can say that with confidence is because I know that God's got it. I also do it to remind myself that as a man and as a leader, I may not like the problem or the issue that has come up—and I may not have even caused it—but it is my position to address it, carry it, and cover those facing it in the best way that I can.

Three fingers.

I've got it.

You've got it.

Try it some time.

But remember that those three fingers work only if you are properly aligned under God's overarching kingdom rule in your life.

First Corinthians 10:31 tells us that whatever we do—whether it is simply eating or drinking—we are to do it for the glory of God. To be aligned under God is to follow this principle in the seemingly mundane as well as in the exciting areas of life. Alignment is to consciously ask yourself what God thinks, says, or wants you to do about this. What will bring Him glory?

A kingdom man is every woman's dream because when he functions according-ing to the principles of God's kingdom, she can rest under his covering.

She can hear him say, *I've got it*, and when she does, she can relax.

As a man, you are responsible. You are to take full responsibility to rule to the best of your ability for the betterment of yourself and all others within your domain. That doesn't mean that you are personally obligated to solve every issue, but it does mean that you are obligated to oversee it being solved if it falls within your realm of influence and authority.

> *She can hear him say,* I've got it, *and when she does, she can relax.*

Men, also remember that *rule* does not mean domination or control; it means leading with wisdom for others. And when you do, as we will see in the next chapter, you are to remember your call to greatness. Men, you were created to be great. You were made for it. It is yours for the taking. Too many men either don't realize this, or they don't know how to get it.

Yet, as a kingdom man, greatness is your destiny.

3

A MAN'S CALL
TO GREATNESS

Nothing can compare to the electricity that permeates the air, saturated with the smell of sweat, as towering men battle head-to-head and hand-to-hand in search for nothing but the net. As the longest-acting chaplain for any NBA team, having served the NBA Dallas Mavericks for over three decades, I've become acutely familiar with the feel and smell of this atmosphere as if it were a part of me. It is both rousing and disarming at the same time. I love it.

You can't help but recognize it as soon as you enter the arena. The air hangs thick with anticipation and hunger, consuming anyone who walks into the presence of the players and coaching staff. To say that passion dominates the mood would be an understatement. It is more like a pure ache for greatness.

When the Mavericks made it to the finals in 2011, two teams with five men on the court unapologetically sought to prove which was the better. They were men on a quest—men with one goal, and that goal was nothing short of declaring to the entire world their greatness.

While women fantasize about relationships, men fantasize about greatness. While women fantasize about cuddling, men fantasize about conquering. As men, we want to *do* something. We crave significance, influence, and impact. This desire for greatness shows up in the sports we play, the wilds we roam, or the movies we watch. A woman might enjoy a chick flick with a nice soft romantic storyline, but men—most men at least—want war. We want to see the blood, the battle, the fight, the intrigue, and we want to feel the rush of the chase. We set out to slay the dragon, storm the castle, and rescue the beauty in distress. We are men. Anything less would be ordinary, and men do not yearn for ordinary.

Men long to be great.

Not only do we long to be great, but we also desire to be recognized as great.

We set out to slay the dragon, storm the castle, and rescue the beauty in distress.

No player on the winning NBA championship team ever turns down his ring. He claims it and wears it so everyone will know what he did. In fact, there are men who won the championship twenty years ago who will still wear their rings. Even though so much time has passed, they wear it because they want others to know that they are great.

When a man walks around with a beautiful woman on his arm, you know what he could be thinking. He might be wanting as many men as possible to see him because he wants others to know that he got her, that he was the warrior who won the beauty's heart.

In fact, so strong is a man's desire for greatness that he may attempt to experience it through someone else. As I mentioned earlier, a common way you see this is when a man shows up in a jersey with another man's name on it—and it is always the number of a player who is considered to be great. Rarely will you see a man wearing a kicker's jersey or a special team player's jersey. Normally, a man will purchase—and pay a large amount—to wear a jersey of the MVP, the quarterback, or another great player on the team.

Whether we feel comfortable enough to admit it in spiritual circles, men want to be great.

I'll admit it; I don't mind—I want to be great.

And if you were brutally honest, I would bet that you also want to be great.

But what may surprise you, and what I would like to suggest, is that far from what we often hear in the biblical teaching on servanthood and humility is that God wants you to be great as well.

Not only does God want you to be great in His kingdom, but He has also destined you for it.

Greatness is maximizing your potential for the glory of God and the good of others. The apostle Paul urged those under his influence when he wrote to the church at Thessalonica to "excel still more" in how they obeyed God's commands (1 Thessalonians 4:1). He urged the Corinthians to always abound in the work of the Lord (1 Corinthians 15:58) and to seek greatness in all that they did since all that they did, according to 1 Corinthians 10:31, was to be done to glorify God.

Men, I want you to experience this truth.

Hear me when I say this—it is okay to want greatness. That is not something you have to mumble when no one is listening or an idea you have to check at the church door. I realize that it may seem to fly in the face of what you have heard as a call to be meek, humble, and a servant of all, but authentic greatness never negates any of those characteristics. In fact, authentic greatness includes the true definition of all of them.

The Strength of Meekness

Meekness is not walking around with a sunken chest, head down, and doing everything you're asked to do by those within your sphere of influence. That is not meekness at all. That is, rather, the world's attempt to cage and emasculate a male. It is the enemy's strategy to castrate men's drive and sideline the starters on God's kingdom team. By painting complacency as a virtue and mediocrity as a goal, Satan has lulled the hearts of men asleep.

The true definition of meekness does not negate hunger or dismiss thirst. Neither does it remove pure unadulterated passion. Keep in mind, gentlemen, that passion, in and of itself, is not a bad thing. It simply means desire. Desire becomes bad only when it is wrongfully directed.

However, what Satan has done is contort what God has said in an attempt to twist the truth into a reality that is no longer recognizable, just as he did with Eve in the garden. Distorting the truth is exactly what Satan continues to do with regard to greatness in connection with meekness. Meekness is not weakness, as many have been led to believe. Meekness simply means submitting your power to a higher Control—it means submitting yourself to God's kingdom rule.

Numbers 12:3 tells us that Moses was a meek man. In fact, Moses was the meekest man: "Now the man Moses was very humble, more than any man who was on the face of the earth." Yet Moses, the meekest man during his time, led one of the bravest and greatest flights to freedom. Only the likes of Charlton Heston could play this man on the big screen. Moses was a powerful man potent with both influence and significance.

Because Moses was able to submit himself to divine authority, God was able to do great things in him and through him. God made Moses a great man. Yet Moses was considered meek because he was willing to serve the purposes of God to reflect the glory of God, rather than his own.

Men, what you never want to do in your desire to be great is to try to steal or usurp God's glory. That is a crucial principle. Take a moment to underline that. Because to attempt to steal or usurp God's glory is the fastest way of not only stalling your bid for greatness, but also reversing it. To do so is to follow in the footsteps of Pharaoh. You remember what Pharaoh said when Moses told Pharaoh that God had sent Moses to let God's people go. Pharaoh said no. He said, in essence, "This is my job, my career, my financial well-being at stake, and I call the shots here. I'm in charge."

> *God is not opposed to greatness. God is opposed to pride.*

Anytime you take a Pharaoh mentality about what God has given you or is asking you to do, that is a power approach to greatness, not meekness. And when a power play is made before God, as it was with Pharaoh, God will quickly "ungreat" you. God ultimately reduced Pharaoh to nothing through the plagues and disintegration of his army because he had the wrong approach to greatness. Pharaoh was unwilling to submit himself to divine authority. However, Moses, when he placed himself under God, witnessed the supernatural invade the natural, thus causing Moses' name to go down in history as great.

Men, God is not opposed to greatness. God is opposed to pride. Big difference. Unfortunately, it is a difference not widely understood or embraced.

God Wants You to Be Great

God wants men to be great so much so that in Genesis 18:17–18, God refers to Abraham as not only a great man but also a great nation. The passage says, "The LORD said, 'Shall I hide from Abraham what I am about to do, since Abraham will surely become a great and mighty nation, and in him all the nations of the earth will be blessed.'"

Earlier in Genesis 12:2, God said directly to Abraham, "I will bless you, and make your name great."

In 2 Samuel 7:9, God echoes these thoughts to David when He says, "I have been with you wherever you have gone and have cut off all your enemies from before you; and I will make you a great name, like the names of the great men who are on earth."

Keep in mind that this was God talking. God was the one telling Abraham and David that He planned to make their names great. God was going to see to it that their names be etched in stone. God would make sure that these men would not have just come here, been here, and then left here. God would make sure that these men would forever be known as great.

Yet before we go any further, I want to pause because I can hear your concern. I hear what you are saying. You are saying, "But, Tony, that's Abraham. That's David. Those *are* great men. That's not me. I am just an ordinary man. God never said that to me."

Oh, but you are wrong.

He did.

In fact, Jesus did, in John 14:12, "Truly, truly, I say to you, he who believes in Me, the works that I do, he will do also; and greater works than these he will do."

That is not a verse we hear preached on too frequently throughout Christendom. But I am not sure why. It is a pretty straightforward truth. Maybe the majority of our preachers have a difficult time believing that something that sounds so good could actually be true. Yet Jesus said plainly that, if you believe in Him, you are going to do stuff that even He didn't get to do on earth. That is a powerful reality that I don't want you to miss. That is a kingdom truth. Not only will you do the great things that Jesus did, but you will also do even greater things.

Jesus never traveled more than a few hundred miles from the place of His birth during His earthly ministry. Yet the gospel has been spread around the world by men who have gone on to do *greater works* on earth.

Now, if Jesus said that you will do "greater works" than He did, then evidently God does not have a problem with greatness. Neither does He have a problem with the recognition of greatness, as we saw earlier when He said He would make both Abraham's and David's names great. Anytime God makes a name great, that means He is recognizing greatness.

Therefore, if in trying to be spiritual, you have shrunk away from your innate desire for significance, I want you to know that, in doing so, you have walked right into the enemy's trap. The enemy doesn't want you to realize that true greatness involves analyzing your gifts, talents, skills, and capacity in God's name and for His glory, and then maximizing them in an effort to expand your impact on others.

God's agenda is to advance His kingdom down the field of life, and to do so, He is looking for men who will rise to the occasion in their bid for greatness. Yet to rise to the occasion to be great, you must first allow yourself, release yourself, and give yourself permission to want it. You were made for greatness. It is okay to want it. In fact, it is more than okay—it is a mandate.

Far too many men are satisfied with being on the practice squad. Far too many men are satisfied with just being okay, with getting by, or living a mundane and ordinary life. Many, if not most, of the problems that we are facing today are because men are thinking too small. They are either not thinking about greatness at all, or they are thinking about it according to the world's grid for greatness.

Imagine if some thieves broke into a store but didn't steal a thing. They just exchanged the tags. They took a $12,000 tag off a Rolex and put it on a Timex. They took the Timex tag of $99 and put it on the Rolex. Imagine they did this with everything in the store. The next day people would come in and buy a bunch of stuff, spending a lot of money on the worthless items and little money on the expensive ones.

We live in a culture that has switched the tags on greatness. It has put a lot of value on the flashy lifestyle while putting only $99 on character. Our culture has put a lot of value on cars and careers but only ten cents on integrity, family, and impact.

God stands in the locker room of our souls with a personal bid for greatness, as long as that greatness comes under His authority and is expressed in an effort to reflect His glory. This is something that the world doesn't necessarily say is valuable but something that eternity has deemed as priceless. Understanding the value of true greatness is the key to experiencing all you were destined to be.

Greatness for the Greater Good

When James and John, known as the Sons of Thunder, sought a place of honor in Christ's kingdom, the other ten disciples gave them a difficult time for expressing their desire for significance. However, Jesus never corrected the two men for what they wanted. After all, He knew how they were formed. He knew what was inside of them. He knew that they were men and desiring greatness in the kingdom of God was not wrong. Jesus corrected them only for how they wanted to go about accomplishing it. "You know that the rulers of the Gentiles lord it over them, and *their* great men exercise authority over them. It is not this way among you, but whoever wishes to become great among you shall be your servant" (Matthew 20:25–26).

Jesus didn't tell the men not to wish to be great. He didn't tell them not to desire significance, influence, and the ability to make a lasting impact. Jesus just told them not to try to get it the same way that the Gentiles did. The Gentiles exercised greatness through lording it over others. They displayed their greatness in power plays and politics, much like our world does today. We live in a power-driven world. Men rule by intimidation, fear-tactics, and leverage. But Jesus said, "It is not that way among you." The rulers of God's kingdom are much different from the rulers of the world, as are their strategies. Jesus didn't diminish a man's need for greatness; He simply defined the way a man ought to get it, which is through service. True greatness is outward-focused and others-driven. It is not dominance, but rather dominion that benefits those around you.

If a running back were to grab the ball and never relinquish it for the remainder of the game because he enjoyed the power he felt when he had it, he would not be using his position to serve the greater needs of the team. The greatest player on any team, whether a corporate, family, ministry, or sports team, is the player who makes certain that his contribution best fits within the goals and strategies of the team. That doesn't mean that he can't stand out or that he can't have his own plays to execute as an individual. It simply means that whatever he does must be done in concert with and in service of the greater good. Greatness is not just a position or a title, but how that position or title plays out in conjunction with the overall goal.

Think about the moon; it has no light of its own. What we see when we witness the grandeur of the moon at night is simply a reflection of the light of the sun. While God has created you to be great, your greatness must always be a reflection of His own. God's greatness was demonstrated clearly through His Son who "did not come to be served, but to serve, and to give His life a ransom for many" (Matthew 20:28). In other words, your greatness ought to be making the lives within your sphere of influence better, not worse. Your greatness ought to inspire other men because they see your impact for good in the lives of others.

Keep in mind that greatness will look different for each of us based on our positions, personalities, and potential. Achieving greatness doesn't mean your name will always be the one in lights on the scoreboard.

When Drew Brees beat Dan Marino's single season passing record on Monday Night Football (December 26, 2011), he made sure to let the entire team know this wasn't only about him. "This record isn't about one person," Brees said in his locker room speech. Then he went on to thank the team, the coaching staff, and all the others involved. It was because of their greatness that he was enabled to do what he did.[1]

Achieving greatness means maximizing all that you are destined to be for the glory of God and for the good of others. One of the greatest players on a football team is the punter. If the punter does not consistently give the opposing team the worst possible field position, the game can change. Momentum can change. The score can change. The outcome can change.

Yet how many fans know the name of the punter on a football team? But known or unknown, he still needs to be great.

Known or unknown, you need to be great.

Greatness for a kingdom man begins by aligning yourself with God's kingdom agenda to benefit others. You must first make the decision that not only do you want greatness, but that you are also going to pursue it according to God's methods. That's where it starts. Now, I understand that making that decision might be difficult for some of you. Perhaps you feel as if life's circumstances have dealt you a raw hand and all odds are against you. It could be different reasons for different men. Perhaps you are facing racial marginalization, or perhaps you were raised without a father or a positive male role model. It could be that you are living in a financial hole, or maybe your coworkers or boss are not playing fair. Maybe your family is currently in shambles or you have already set the tone for passive leadership in your home.

Whatever the odds, never let the odds determine your destiny. God has destined you for greatness. Jesus said that if you believe in Him, you *will do* greater works than He did. He didn't say that you might do them. He didn't even say that you could do them. Jesus said that, if you believe, you *will* do them.

You will.

4

THE POWER OF ONE REAL MAN

One Old Testament man believed in his destiny of greatness and it showed up in his actions, despite overwhelming odds. If I were to poll everyone reading right now, I would suspect that not even a quarter of you have heard of him. This man didn't get much airtime compared to the likes of Samson, David, or Joshua. Even Jabez came in with more words at sixty-nine compared to this man's measly forty-six. (See 1 Chronicles 4:9–10 and Judges 3:31; 5:6.)

Yet the two lessons found in the two verses about this man, if you will grasp them, will not only transform your life, but will also transform our world. As you will see, it took only one real man named Shamgar to save the entire nation of Israel.

By way of introduction, since you may not know much about him, Shamgar's story takes place in the time of the judges. The time of the judges, as you may well know, is a time of chaos followed by peace followed by chaos. It would be akin to what we call a postmodern era. A postmodern era is basically when relativism rules. There are no absolutes or any guidelines to govern individuals or the society. Several times in the era of the judges, much like what we are experiencing in our contemporary culture today, the book of Judges recorded that "everyone did what was right in his own eyes" (Judges 21:25). What was right for one person wasn't necessarily right for another. Each person did his own thing without any over-arching rule or governance. As you might imagine, it was a terrifying time in which to live.

We know that it was a terrifying time when Shamgar lived because the details in one of the two verses about this man tell us so. Judges 5:6 states, "In the days of Shamgar the son of Anath, in the days of Jael, the highways were deserted, and travelers went by roundabout ways."

People weren't traveling the main thoroughfares. And if they did travel at all, they had to go out of their way through the back roads. The reason why a nation resorts to traveling its back roads is when that nation has lost control of its front ones. To be out in public, at this time, was to put your life at risk. This was a day of terrorism when marauding bands of irresponsible men created havoc, jeopardizing both women and children. Thuggery dominated the land to such a degree that people had to walk around the outer edges of the cities to get where they needed to go.

> *This was a day of terrorism when marauding bands of irresponsible men created havoc.*

But then there is Shamgar. His name alone sounds like a superhero. Pronounce it slowly: *Sh-am-ga-rr.* You can almost hear the growl at the end. There is power in that name. But more than his name, Shamgar himself had power. The other verse about him tells us the extent of the power found in one real man. Judges 3:31 says, "After him came Shamgar the son of Anath, who struck down six hundred Philistines with an oxgoad; and he also saved Israel."

Shamgar, whom we know today as the third minor judge in the history of Israel, did not start out that way. Shamgar became a judge. And while Scripture doesn't delve into the details of Shamgar's life, we can make some conclusions based on the cultural norms of the agrarian and economically challenged society he lived in. One is that Shamgar started in an ordinary existence. Judging from his use of his oxgoad, we might assume that Shamgar was like most of the honest men of that day—trying to provide for his family as a farmer. Shamgar's oxgoad would have been like everyone else's oxgoad—a long eight-foot pole with a sharp end on it. The other end of the oxgoad served as a chisel.

In biblical days when a farmer followed an ox plowing a field and the ox got sluggish, he would goad the ox to get it moving again. Likewise, when the farmer came across a root that was not coming up out of the ground as it should, he would dig the chisel deep under it to remove it. An oxgoad was an essential farming tool.

Shamgar was not a military man. Neither was he a politician. But what is critical to learn from the life of this man was that Shamgar did not wait until things were "easy" to do something on behalf of his nation. Shamgar didn't wait until he became great to do something great. He didn't put off until next week what he needed to do that day. Shamgar saved the entire nation of Israel, and he did it as a farmer.

Lesson Number One: Stop Making Excuses

Men, the first lesson about the power of one real man is to stop making excuses. No more delaying what needs to be done until you feel you are in a position to do it. Rather than whining that you are not a judge yet, or that you haven't been promoted yet, or that you don't have all of the resources you feel you need yet, discover what you can do right now and do it. Stop making excuses.

So many men today are flooding the airwaves with excuses for why they are not taking care of business. They are sitting around reminiscing over bygone days of glory when they cut their first deal, made the team, or closed their first major purchase.

Men, I understand that life may not be what you want it to be. I understand that life has challenges and it doesn't come quite as easily as it once did in the sandlot, at the diamond, or in less challenging times. But the first lesson in becoming a kingdom man of influence and impact is to stop making excuses. Maybe you are not where you thought you should be. It could be that life has dealt you a bad blow. You didn't have a father. You didn't have a positive male role model. You have made mistakes in your home, with your finances, or you have jumped from career to career failing to build momentum along the way. I get that. I understand. But what can you do now?

One of the reasons why we have so many ineffective Christian men in our nation today is because men are waiting for something to happen before they will do what they can do where they are. If you are a farmer and that is all you know how to do, then you need to ask God how He wants you to use your farming to influence and impact the realm you live in now.

You may not be in your dream job or dream situation, and you may literally be stuck away in some obscure location, but take a tip from a man named Shamgar. Shamgar was a farmer. In fact, Shamgar was a farmer in a time when his whole world was in chaos. If the roads are shut down because of gang activity, how do you think a farmer is going to distribute his goods? His entire marketing and distribution channels had been closed. Shamgar's economic security lay in shambles. Yet that did not stop him from saving an entire nation with the tool he had. Shamgar was dissatisfied with the culture in which he lived, and rather than sit back and bemoan it like an armchair quarterback, Shamgar decided to do something about it. Shamgar decided to save Israel.

> *Don't wait until you become a big shot to do big shot things.*

Keep in mind that Shamgar was a farmer before he ever became a judge. Yet had he made the excuse that he was only a farmer, he would have never become a judge. I guarantee it. Shamgar became a judge because he delivered a nation. Men, don't wait until you become great to say, "Hey, now I am going to do something." Don't wait until you become a big shot to do big shot things. Shamgar didn't wait until he had a bigger tool, a bigger weapon, a bigger name, or a bigger army. Shamgar didn't make excuses for not having any of that. He saw a need, and he met that need with the resources he had at his disposal.

What Will You Do With What You've Got?

As you might imagine, with a radio and television ministry that reaches millions, I will frequently get young pastors who come up to me after I speak somewhere or try to catch me by phone or at the church with one question in mind. They want to know how they can get what I have. These pastors approach me to ask for the secret. They want to know, "Tony, how can I get that too?"

I always reply, "Tell me when was the last time you preached at a prison. Or when was the last time you sat down with a group of ninth-grade boys and explained to them what it will take for them to become a man." Most men don't like that response. That was not what they were looking for when they posed the question. Yet, as in any career or ministry, if you aren't willing to start at the beginning and be responsible where you are, then how do you expect God to give you more? We wouldn't do that with our own children. Why should He? If you gave your child a dollar bill and he lost it, would you then give him two? Of course not. First you want to see what your child can do with the dollar bill before you go and double it. It is important that men stop making excuses for why they aren't maximizing everything within the sphere of where they are and then blaming God for not giving them more.

I didn't start out on the radio or on television. No one does. I started out as a fifteen-year-old boy preaching with my father and handing out tracts on street corners every week in urban Baltimore, Maryland. In fact, sometimes I would literally climb up on top of a parked car and preach to anyone passing by. My dad still jokes with me about that. He says that I wanted to make sure everyone was able to hear.

Then, after I did that for a while, my father let me graduate to preach at the local prison. By the time I got to college, I was preaching at bus stops. Most Friday nights you would find me preaching to anyone who would listen at the bus stops in Atlanta. I knew only one sermon at the time: "Repent, and be saved in the name of Jesus Christ." And I preached it every week. There was no honorarium. There was no pay. Half the time, no one even looked at me—or if they did, it was to glare. But based on where I was at that point in my life, that was the best congregation that I could locate. Churches certainly weren't inviting me to come preach to them. Yet God had called me to preach, so I wasn't about to wait for a church to invite me. I had to go create one.

Eventually, after Bible college and seminary, I ended up with ten families sitting in my home each Sunday morning and looking at me to be their pastor. Still not much by the world's standards, and certainly not enough to even pay our rent. But that is what I had, so that is what I did. I didn't sit around saying, "Well, this is just ten families, and a good number of them are relatives. How am I even going to pay my bills? I need to get another job and wait until I have a larger building with more lives to impact before I start preaching." No, I made it my goal to impact those ten families for the kingdom of God in any and every way that I could. Every Sunday morning, with ten families in my home, I would stand up at a makeshift podium and go line by line through my study notes and outline that I had prepared for that week. And every week for several years I would go door-to-door taking the gospel to people in the urban neighborhood I was trying to reach. Eventually, ten families turned into a hundred, and a hundred families turned into a thousand, and a thousand families turned into nearly ten thousand.

Men, I want you to grab hold of this principle because it will change your life—if you will simply make the most of where you are, God will do the rest. He is watching to see what you will do first with what He has already given you when no one else is paying that much attention.

What Shamgar did as a farmer was take the limited resources that he had, an oxgoad, and put it in the hands of God for the purposes of God. By doing so, he multiplied his possibilities. All Shamgar owned was an oxgoad, but the key is that he knew how to use it. He looked at the thing in his hand and determined that the sharp end could be a flying missile or a spear. When he viewed his limited resources differently, he saw that they could be used for more than what he had originally imagined.

> *If you will simply make the most of where you are, God will do the rest.*

Never let your limitations limit what God can do with you. When you look a little closer at what you have, you may discover, like Shamgar, that you have more than enough to accomplish God's plan for you. After all, Moses merely had a staff, but he opened up the Red Sea. All David had was a slingshot and five smooth stones, but he delivered his nation from the enemy. All Samson had was the jawbone of a donkey, but he slew the Philistines. All a lad had was two fish and five barley loaves, but God used it to feed five thousand men. Never look at only what you have. Look at what it can become.

All Michael Jordan had was a ball, but the man is worth megamillions because of it. All Hank Aaron had was a hammer—his bat—but that spawned successful businesses throughout the South, endorsements, statues of him outside of several ballparks, a ballpark named after him in Alabama, and a ticket into the Baseball Hall of Fame.[1] Yes, you may be limited in resources or even in skills, but while God doesn't always call the equipped, He always equips the called. What you have is all you need to do what God has destined you for right now. Use it.

Shamgar was a farmer. Not only that, but Shamgar was a farmer with the odds stacked against him. Despite that, he didn't make excuses. He didn't wait until he had a degree in Judge-ship. He simply used what he had.

Lesson Number Two: Advance One Step at a Time

After you stop making excuses, the next principle you can learn from the life of Shamgar is to advance one step at a time. Because Shamgar was a farmer, he knew this principle probably like he knew the back of his hand. He knew that planting one kernel of wheat would produce a stalk with three heads on it, and that each head would include roughly fifteen to thirty new kernels, representing nearly one hundred new kernels in all. Shamgar knew that when he planted those one hundred kernels, they would eventually produce ten thousand kernels, which when planted would then represent a million new kernels. It is the principle of multiplication. We use it in business. We use it in strategy planning. We use it in evangelism and missions. But since Shamgar was so familiar with the principle of multiplication, he used it in battle.

When we looked at Judges 3:31 earlier, we read that Shamgar killed six hundred men. If you read that too quickly, you might not stop to think that one man killing six hundred men really doesn't make much sense. Not only is it illogical, but it also doesn't seem possible. I don't care if he has a machine gun in his hand, he may get a few men, but one man up against six hundred will eventually go down.

So how did Shamgar topple six hundred men and still remain standing?

By taking them down one man at a time.

It is the same way you lose weight one pound at a time, write a book one chapter at a time, and win the Super Bowl one game at a time. That's how you do it. You don't do it all at once. If you tried, you wouldn't get far at all.

Since Judges 5 tells us that no one was traveling the main highways in the land at that time, we can assume that the Israelites' enemy was operating in gangs as units. That is the only way that they could cover so much ground at one time. If all the highways were dangerous, then that means there was a platoon over here and a platoon over there to intimidate the travelers coming from any direction. So when Shamgar performed his reconnaissance, he targeted a group at a time. He didn't attack all six hundred at once. He attacked one gang here then another gang over there. He picked them off in pieces.

One of the major excuses men will make when facing what seems like an insurmountable challenge or goal is to say that they cannot do all of it, so they don't do anything at all. But like the kernel of wheat planted in the ground, if you will simply take each challenge one step at a time, one day at a time, one project at a time, you will be amazed at where you eventually wind up.

Many men want to become a millionaire by playing the lottery. But each of us had the opportunity to become a millionaire by simply saving $100 a month from the time we were 18 and letting that compound with interest. Yet because we don't look long-term or plan much farther beyond what we can see, very few of us will take the small steps necessary toward accomplishing greatness.

> *Few of us will take the small steps necessary toward accomplishing greatness.*

One man saved a nation simply because he didn't attempt to save it all at once. He did what he could where he was with what he had, and soon he had sliced up six hundred. Gentlemen, that is the secret. And it is a powerful secret if you will simply own it and apply it.

Your Pedigree Does Not Determine Your Purpose

But there is one more thing to glean from the life of Shamgar, and it comes from his name. Shamgar's is an unusual name to have attributed to a hero among the Israelites primarily because it is derived from a Hurrian root meaning "Shimig (the god) has given." In addition to his name displaying a clear lack of Hebrew association, his family name did the same. Known as the Son of Anath, Shamgar's family etymology was linked to the Canaanite goddess of war.[2]

Yet, while Shamgar may not have come from the right pedigree in order to be a Hebrew judge, he acted as a Hebrew judge even before he was made one. Shamgar didn't allow his limited resources and unorthodox roots to limit him. And neither should you. No matter where you are starting from, where you have come from, what limitations you face or associations you have been birthed or bred into—God can make you great.

When you choose to seek God and His ways like Shamgar, you no longer have to be held hostage to the definitions of this world. You no longer have to be held hostage to an idea that perhaps you are not smart enough, not fast enough, not well-groomed enough, not talented enough, not influential enough, or not powerful enough to achieve greatness. It is irrelevant what people think or say if God says something different. Jesus said, "He who believes in Me, the works that I do, he will do also; and greater works than these he will do."

Jesus is talking about you.

You have a destiny of greatness. There is something you were created to do. There is something you are passionate about, willing to be committed to, and longing to seek. It is your destiny.

Yes, I realize that it may be late for some of you. You may have lost it, forgotten it, or never have even known what it is. Maybe the dream of your destiny was ripped from you in your childhood, by your mate, by your circumstances, or through pain. But every man has a destiny. Men were created for dominion—to rule with wisdom over the realm in which they are placed (keeping in mind that ruling means leading according to the will of God and always for the good of those within your realm of influence).

There may be six hundred Philistines out there for you to conquer, but you will never get them if you are waiting to do it after you leave the farm. God is calling you now. He has something for you to use now. You may not know what it is, but you will discover it if you will seek Him. You have an oxgoad—the one thing you can maximize if you are just willing to try.

Gentlemen, for us to move forward as individuals in our homes, churches, and communities, and as a nation, it will require more than the faint of heart. It will require men of courage who will rise to the occasion within the realm where they have been placed.

You Are the One

The box office smash *The Matrix* centers on an ordinary man by the name of Thomas Anderson. By day, Anderson is a computer programmer in a company that not only uses him, but also equally bores him. By night Anderson tries to make extra money as a computer hacker, which isn't much better of a life. Yet one day Anderson is ushered to a point of decision. Anderson is led to a place where it is explained to him that behind the physical, visible realm in which he lives resides another realm that he cannot yet see. This other realm that he cannot see actually dictates what goes on in the physical realm that he can see.

Anderson is also told that the physical realm in which he lives has been positioned and fated for disaster through forces in the invisible realm unless some-one enters it and intervenes. Someone like him, specially created for this moment in time. Yet to enter this other realm, Anderson has to make a choice. He can't live in both realms at the same time. Anderson has to relinquish the ordinary and predictable to embrace the extraordinary and powerful. And he is to demonstrate that choice by swallowing a red pill, which will then immediately transport him into his new reality.

Thomas Anderson chooses to swallow the red pill.

When he swallowed the pill, he was no longer simply Thomas Anderson. Rather, he got a new name. His new name was Neo. Along with his new name came a new set of clothes and a new set of abilities and powers to do what he never could have done before. He could fight a hundred men at one time. Fly into the ionosphere. Stop a thousand bullets—with his mind. Neo could do anything he wanted in this new realm. He even got the girl, a beautiful woman named Trinity who believed in him and had dreamed of his coming into her life.

But more important than all of that, Neo discovered his purpose. His signifi-cance. His substance. His reason for being.

Neo had been brought to this new realm because he had been chosen as the one to deliver those who were trapped in the ill-fated environment from where he had come.

Neo was *the one.*

As many of you may know, one film turned into a trilogy. Through the course of battles and wars taking place in them all, Neo eventually conquered the legions assembled against him, a cloned force of millions named Smith. What is even more impressive is that he did it as one man. Neo took them all down by himself.

He was *the one.* [3]

Those films are my favorites not only because of the action and the adventure, but also because of the moral that can transcend the screen and change your life. If we will let it—if you will let it—because like Thomas Anderson, you also have a purpose. Significance. Substance. A reason for being. You have a battle to win. An enemy to conquer. And a realm to deliver.

You are *the one.*

The choice is yours. You can either take the red pill—the pill that has been offered, infused with the power and authority given to you by the blood of Jesus

Christ—and you can be ushered into your call to greatness. Or you can take the other pill, only to live out the remainder of your ordinary existence.

You are *the one*.

You are the one to make a difference in your destiny, your family, church, work, community, our nation, and around the world.

No one will force you to step up to your calling. . . . It's your choice. No one will force you to take the red pill. It's your choice. A choice you have to make that will determine if you are going to remain fixated and focused on this realm—an earthly man—or if you are going to operate from and engage the powers of another realm—bringing that other realm's authority to bear on Earth—through choosing to become a kingdom man.

Be *the one*.

> *No one will force you to step up to your calling. . . . It's your choice.*

5

Aligning Yourself for Impact

With only seconds left on the clock and no time-outs remaining in the 1958 NFL Championship Game, the Baltimore Colts faced a critical decision: go for a touchdown or kick a field goal. Even though Colts quarterback Johnny Unitas had been nothing short of perfect, moving the ball 62 yards in what is one of the most famous drives in NFL history, the Colts still needed to score in the last seven seconds.[1] Down by 3 to the New York Giants and with the ball on the 13-yard line, it could be that Colts Coach Weeb Ewbank remembered the failed fourth and goal earlier in the half[2] when he had told Unitas to "go for it."[3] Rather than scoring, the Colts were pummeled by the Giants for a 4-yard loss, turning the ball over on downs.

Even though a field goal would only tie the Championship Game, it was better than a loss. As the seconds ticked away, Colts kicker Steve Myhra followed Ewbank's orders and made a mad dash to get into position. Myhra's kick went sailing, splitting the uprights, and sent the NFL into a panic. The score was now 17–17.[4]

Up until then, regular season NFL games that ended in a tie remained just that. But this was a Championship Game. What's more, this was a Championship Game in a sport that was struggling to gain notoriety and fans, having played a distant runner-up in popularity to the national pastime of baseball. Players had battled and fought year after year with bruises, concussions, and even a broken leg[5] in this particular game, only to gain little national respect and even less of a paycheck. Without the economic support of a strong fan base, the future of professional football in America looked as if it might turn into an awkward fumble.

But this nationally televised Championship Football Game had proven to be an eyes-glued-to-the-screen one so far, no doubt whetting the appetite of a potential fan base for more. And now—having ended in a tie—none of the forty-five million[6] viewers could bring themselves to look away.

Myself included.

Having grown up in Baltimore, I felt this was my team. These were my Colts. My childhood sports hero, Colts halfback Lenny Moore, had been one of the first black men to claim the honor of NFL Rookie of the Year[7] just a few seasons before. My eight-year-old eyes stared at the screen with the millions of others. We were all holding our breath and waiting to see what would happen next.

> *Having grown up in Baltimore, I felt this was my team. These were my Colts.*

The coaches and players waited as well.

Then, in an unprecedented move, the officials walked onto the field and announced that the game would go into overtime. For the first time in NFL history, and pretty much a decision made on the spot, a game went to sudden death.[8] I, along with the rest of Baltimore, was glad that it did, because not too many plays later, the Colts converted a third and goal into 6 points,[9] claiming the 1958 NFL Championship title. Since then, that Championship Game has been dubbed "The Greatest Game Ever Played."[10]

I am sure you won't be surprised if I tell you that every able-bodied schoolboy in Baltimore gathered in the alley or at the local park every Saturday after that to play football. I had already made it my habit to play touch football during the week in the alley behind my home and tackle football each Saturday at the local park. But when the Colts clinched not only the 1958 championship but also went on to claim the 1959 championship as well,[11] boys showed up in droves at our games—each one trying his hand at being a Moore, a Unitas, or a Raymond Berry.

I don't know what it is about boys and heroes, but you can ask any man who it was that he looked up to as a kid, and he'll start rattling off a name, or two, or ten. The accomplishments of men inspire boys to become like them. The back-to-back Colts' championships undoubtedly planted dreams in the hearts and souls of boys throughout Baltimore. As a result, more than most of my friends wanted to grow up to play football.

I did, too.

But there was something else that I wanted to be when I grew up even more. I wanted to be a man.

Being a Man

Something about being a man rouses me. Whatever it is, it never fails to wake me up each morning with a drive to solve the current challenge or conquer the latest quest. The authority and responsibility that God has uniquely established in biblical manhood sometimes blows my mind. If we, as men, could ever fully comprehend all that God has not only intended for us but has also provided for us, we would not only improve our own lives, as well as our families', but we would also impact our churches, communities, and the entire world.

Unfortunately, though, most men don't seem to get it. A large portion of their manhood has been forfeited simply because these men do not understand, or live according to, the theological perspective on what it means to be a kingdom man. Many false definitions of manhood exist, including the following:

Passive Man: A male is who is unable or unwilling to take the leadership role that God has assigned him to have.

Domineering Man: A male who thinks manhood is measured by his ability to emotionally and/or physically force compliance to his demands.

Sexual Man: A male who measures his manhood by the amount of women he can conquer.

Corporate Man: A male who defines his manhood by the amount of time he invests in his career and/or by the amount of money he can accrue.

Irresponsible Man: A male who refuses to provide properly for the well-being of those under his care.

Hedonistic Man: A male who lives for self-gratifying pleasure at the expense of those around him.

Only when a man functions as a biblical kingdom man will he experience the fullness of his destiny. Yet when a man does not live according to the biblical definition of manhood, it shows up in his own life and in the lives under his influence and care.

Not too long ago I took my car into the dealership for its routine oil change and other maintenance. Shortly after I had dropped off my car, I got a call from the dealership telling me that they had discovered another issue that was wrong with my vehicle: My tires were not wearing evenly. The problem, though, wasn't with my tires. My tires were fine. In fact, my tires had been top-of-the-line quality tires. My problem, as the mechanic explained it to me, was with my vehicle's alignment. He told me, "Even if I replace your tires, Tony, if I don't fix the alignment, you will end up with the same problem on your new tires."

Addressing my worn out tires by replacing them would not have solved my problem. All that would have done is waste more money in purchasing new tires that would wind up in the same condition, if not worse. The problem with my tires was that my car's wheels were no longer aligned properly.

When we look around our world today, we can see a lot of wear and tear. There is a lot of wear and tear on women who are being misused, abused, or neglected. There is a lot of wear and tear on children who are being forgotten, misled, or turned loose. There is a lot of wear and tear on churches that split, sit stagnant, or fail to develop men who grasp the abundant life or the high call to discipleship. There is a lot of wear and tear in our communities and our nation as the economic, educational, racial, criminal, social, and health care wars dismantle our stability.

Yet we cannot resolve any of these issues without first addressing the cause of them. Because if all we do is replace one wife with a new one, one career with a new one, one education or health care system with a new one, one identity with a new one, one church with a new one, or pawn the children out to surrogate sitters found in computer games, television, social circles, or school, we will end up with the exact same problems.

Men, we don't have a wife, family, kids, community, or job problem. We have a man problem. As harsh as this may sound, it boils down to you. And it boils down to me as well. It boils down to us. Because if a man is out of alignment with God's prescription for kingdom manhood, it not only messes him up, but it can also mess up anyone or everyone else who comes into contact with him, especially if they fall under his authority.

One of the major causes of the crises we are facing today in so many arenas is that men are not aligning themselves with the purposes of God's kingdom. Until that alignment is made right, wear and tear will only perpetuate itself, resulting in counseling and pastoral offices like my own continuing to be flooded with the fallout.

Which Hood Are You In?

Many men are out of alignment with God because they have gotten their definition of manhood from illegitimate, inadequate, or errant sources, including the media, male influencers in their life, the home they grew up in, or even music. But there is more to being a man than what these sources may say. Being a kingdom man involves exercising authority and responsibility along with wisdom and compassion. A kingdom man intentionally aligns his life, choices, thoughts, and actions under the lordship of Jesus Christ. Being a kingdom man involves more than merely a box checked on your birth certificate that indicates male. In fact, a man can actually fall into three categories of boxes. I call them the three "hoods."

All men begin in the first category of *male-hood*. Male-hood simply has to do with sexual identity. Male-hood used to be discovered at the time of birth, but with ultrasound technology, it can become clear earlier whether a baby in the womb falls into the category of male-hood. Unfortunately, though, some men stay defined by nothing more than their sexual identity their entire lives.

A second category that all men pass through, and many remain in, is *boyhood*. Boyhood is based on immaturity coupled with dependency. One thing that is true of any boy is that he is immature. Boys do not make wise decisions on their own, which is fine—*if you are seven*. The difficulty today, though, is that we have many men who are no longer seven but who are still looking for somebody else to take care of them. They are looking for someone else to be responsible for them. They are looking for someone else to clean up their mess—not just physically, but the emotional, financial, or relational messes they leave in their wake as they rush through life making unwise or self-absorbed decisions. Any wife who has to take care of her man is actually taking care of a boy because that is a characteristic of boyhood. While it is the rare woman who will admit her age, it has become the rare man who will act his age, which leaves behind worldly confusion rather than a lasting kingdom impact for good.

> *Boys do not make wise decisions on their own, which is fine—if you are seven.*

A number of marital problems stem from a man's trying to live in both of these first two hoods at the same time—male-hood and boyhood. In this combination, not only is the man irresponsible and dependent, but he also demands sexual fulfillment based on his sexual identity. This leads to conflicting relational standards producing not only confusion in the marriage, but also feelings of being used on the part of the wife. What woman wants to be intimate with someone whom she has to clean up after, wake up for church, and babysit. Her rationale is that if he can be a man in bed, then why can't he be a man in the living room, at the office, with the finances, as a father, or in the marital relationship? And it is a fair question to ask.

Yet not only does a marriage or family suffer when men perpetually remain in the state of boyhood, but the church, community, and country suffer as well. Anytime there is an absence of men—whether that be physically or simply by definition of what it means to be a kingdom man—the impact is like a tsunami.

When God wanted to debilitate the Egyptian stronghold over the Israelites in slavery, His final and most definitive move was to wipe out their firstborn males. In doing so, He essentially wiped out a generation of leaders because firstborn males have historically held the high positions in society. In fact, that reality isn't found only in the annals of ancient Egyptian culture; it plays out in our contemporary society as well.

In *The Birth Order Book,* author Dr. Kevin Leman points out some interesting statistics about firstborn males. Over half of all US presidents were the firstborn males in their families. And out of the original twenty-three astronauts to head up the space program in our nation, all twenty-three classified as firstborn males—twenty-one were firstborn males, and two were men who had been raised as only children. Even the senior pastor role is most often held by firstborn males,[12] and that firstborn CEOs typically out number any of the others in the birth order.[13] By wiping out the firstborn males in ancient Egypt, God not only affected the current state of the nation, but He also affected generations to come.

Unfortunately, with the rise of promiscuity and the inordinate number of children, especially firstborn children, born to single mothers (a nationwide high was reached in the 2010 National Vital Statistics Report of 40.6 percent) we have a country at risk. In chapter 2, we already saw the results of what happens to children who grow up in fatherless homes, and yet 40 percent of all of the children born in America are being brought into fatherless homes—that number being highest for black children at 72 percent.[14] Men, keep in mind, women are not getting themselves pregnant. This is a man problem.

A nation without kingdom men to lead it will succumb to many ills. As revealed in the book of Isaiah, a culture is in trouble when real men are hard to come by. "O My people! Their oppressors are children, and women rule over them. O My people! Those who guide you lead *you* astray and confuse the direction of your paths" (Isaiah 3:12).

An entire society can be subjected to God's wrath, at most, and His lack of blessing, at least, when men abdicate their God-given positions. In Malachi 4:4–6 God told the men what needed to happen to escape His curse: "Remember the law of Moses My servant, *even the* statutes and ordinances which I commanded him in Horeb for all Israel. Behold, I am going to send you Elijah the prophet before the coming of the great and terrible day of the LORD. He will restore the hearts of the fathers to *their* children and the hearts of the children to their fathers, so that I will not come and smite the land with a curse."

As recorded in Ezekiel, God released His judgment on a culture as a direct result of the absence of biblical manhood. God said, "I searched for a man among them who would build up the wall and stand in the gap before

> *When the almighty, omniscient God cannot find a man, it's a real problem.*

Me for the land, so that I would not destroy it; but I found no one" (Ezekiel 22:30). When the almighty, omniscient God cannot find a man, it's a real problem. If a God who knows everything and knows everyone cannot find one man to stand in the gap for an entire nation, then real men must be hard to come by. God's problem wasn't simply in locating a male or finding a boy. God couldn't find a man, according to His definition of manhood.

God's definition of a kingdom man brings a male out of male-hood and out of boyhood and places him in the third category called *manhood*. More specifically, it is in the category of biblical manhood. This is when a man not only understands and embraces, but also fully lives out, the principles and truths in God's Word.

Responsibility is critical. While you can't control the circumstances in your life or those you come into contact with, you always have control over how you respond and what you want to try to achieve in a situation. The year Tony Dungy coached his team the Indianapolis Colts to a win at the Super Bowl, he and I would phone each other regularly for prayer. All throughout the season, we prayed—not just for a winning season, but for God to be glorified through this venue. In fact, I'll never forget Tony calling me the week of the Super Bowl and saying, "Win or lose, this is my prayer—I want to make sure that I make God's name great." And he did.

Tony Dungy's road to the Super Bowl, though, wasn't paved in gold. It was a long, hard road filled with obstacles and challenges. Tony shared once how his father taught him to approach the challenges of life as a man. He, like myself and many others, grew up in a time of racial segregation and separate-but-not-equal schools. Tony's dad worked as a teacher in a school system with unequal tools, unequal equipment, unequal textbooks, unequal facilities, unequal pay, and often even unequal staff. Tony says that his father would always hold to his calling that God had charged him with the task of training the students in an unequal environment on as equal of a level as he could. He said that if his son, Tony, and the other students couldn't go to the other schools that were better equipped to teach children and prepare them for the future, then it was up to him to teach them at that same level in any way that he could.

Tony Dungy says his father taught him never to complain. His father modeled the responsibility of manhood despite opposition. He taught Tony to take care of business as best as you can with the resources that you have. He never asked Tony or the other students to skip over the reality that segregation and racism were an injustice, but he didn't want them spending all of their time focusing on what they couldn't change rather than on being responsible for what they could.

Because of this, Tony said it brought tears to his eyes when a few years ago he and the Indianapolis players drove to the White House to be congratulated by the President of the United States for winning the Super Bowl. Tony's father had taught just miles from the White House in unequal, segregated schools, and here was Tony who had become the first African-American coach to win a Super Bowl. This came about in large part because his father modeled what it meant to take responsibility for what he could control while waiting on God to change the situation of what he could not. His father lived aligned under God and responsible over those within his care.

The difficulties that we face in our individual lives, families, churches, and communities are not fundamentally tied to our personality differences or our situations. The problems that we face today are fundamentally tied to what Adam began in the garden—a lack of alignment. The devil has sought to exploit personality flaws, differences, backgrounds, histories, and relational issues, but the reason why he has had such an open door to twist, turn, and take advantage of those areas is because we are out of alignment. As a result, those we are responsible for under our care have drowned in the wake of our chaos. Alignment is not just a suggestion; men, it is essential to carrying out your divine reason for being.

Women and Children First

On February 26, 1852, at approximately two o'clock in the morning, a British Royal Navy ship, the HMS *Birkenhead*, carrying 643 people suddenly struck a sunken rock off the coast of the appropriately named Point Danger. Having recently left Cape Town, South Africa, the ship was but hours away from its final destination. The iron-hulled, ocean-going paddle steamer carried mostly military personnel, but as was the custom of the day in areas of relative security, a number of wives and children had also come along.

The damage done to the mammoth ship was irreparable, having sliced her bow clean open between the forepeak and the engine room. In fact, within twenty minutes of having struck the rock, the ship broke into a million unsalvageable pieces—sinking into oblivion. But those final twenty minutes were a defining twenty minutes not only for everyone on board the HMS *Birkenhead*, but also for countless lives since.

Only moments after impact, both the captain of the ship, Captain Robert Salmond, along with his right-hand man, Lieutenant-Colonel Alexander Seton, appeared on the deck. With most of the crewmen having had less than a year of military experience, the captain and lieutenant colonel faced the potential for ensuing chaos. An early assessment of the damage made it clear that the ship would go down within minutes. The only hope for survival in the shark-infested waters roughly three miles from land would be the eight lifeboats onboard. Unfortunately, only three of those lifeboats were able to be lowered; the other five didn't have working chains because of damage from exposure to rain.

Lieutenant-Colonel Seton quickly set the tone for order on the ship when everyone first arrived on deck.

History did not record that Seton or Salmond ever used the exact words "women and children first," but everyone who survived the wreck said that they made it perfectly clear who was to get into the three lifeboats first. Precedent on navy or military vessels had been that in times of emergencies during a war, it was every man for himself. But this boat carried that which was precious—women and children. Those in command couldn't have disorder in light of that. First, they filled the boats with the women and the children, and next they followed the protocol known as "Funeral Order," putting the youngest men on first.

Within ten minutes, all three boats had been filled and lowered in order to drift away from the sinking wreck. Yet as the *Birkenhead* lurched, and began to break up for its ultimate demise, the men left on the ship were put in further danger by the sudden falling of the ship's funnel, which had been torn from its base. This led to an increase in anxiety and a temporary break in the remaining line. Seton, knowing full well the downfall of disorder, would have none of that. He quickly shouted for the men to resume their positions. They immediately did.

Yet as the ship began to make its last twists and turns in the eerie calm just before the closing chapter, the men began to panic, threatening to jump overboard and make for the boats. In fact, even Captain Salmond urged the men to jump overboard and swim for the boats.

Certain this would mean the inevitable deaths of the women and children in them, two junior officers, Captain Wright and Captain Girador, raised their swords in the air and shouted for the men to stand fast.

Without hesitation, every man held his place in strong submission, even as the ship broke up beneath them and the waters swallowed the majority of them to their deaths. Only a handful were able to make the three-mile swim to shore, surviving the shark attacks. Most died, including Lieutenant-Colonel Seton and Captain Salmond.

Yet everyone in the three lifeboats survived.

More than a few good men lost their lives that day so that a handful of women and children could keep theirs. Those remaining recounted shortly afterward that even when the ship went down, none of the men struggling to survive in the cold, shark-infested waters made an attempt to approach the boats. The charge had been given. They had been asked to stand fast. And as a result, every woman and child was kept safe.

"Women and children first" instantly became the protocol not only for all future maritime emergencies in Britain, but for many emergencies around the world as well. A history of the 74th Highlanders says the action on the *Birkenhead* "sheds more glory upon those who took part in it than a hundred well-fought battles."[15]

Had frantic men stormed the lifeboats that cold February morning off the coast of Point Danger, it is likely that all passengers, including the men, would have been lost as the boats capsized in the chaos.

Yet because the men were men who honored the kingdom values set before them, not only did the women and children survive, but the men's legacies did as well.

Men, we serve in a kingdom. God is our King. Christ is our head, our leader. And He has asked us to stand fast. He has asked us to give our undivided allegiance to Christ's command through His headship over our lives, regardless of the cost. It is our responsibility as men to see to it that those under our care—those who depend on us and those within our realm of influence—have every opportunity possible for protection, provision, and safety. If we don't give that to them, not only will they end up suffering, but others will suffer, too.

Stand Fast

Although I thoroughly enjoyed watching every minute of the 1958 NFL Championship Game and seeing my hometown Colts secure the title not only one time but also a second time the following year—even as a child I knew I wanted to do something more than just play football. I, like many boys, dreamed of growing up and playing professional football. But something inside of me said, *Whatever you do, Evans, do it right. Be a man. Be a real man.*

When I mentioned my childhood sports hero, football player Lenny Moore, I didn't tell you that he wasn't my only hero. In fact, he wasn't my greatest hero. Rather, there was someone I admired even more. The one I looked up to the most as a schoolboy in Baltimore actually wore a cape rather than a helmet. He flew rather than ran. Some days he went by the name of Clark. Other days he was Superman. As I mentioned earlier, I wanted to be a man. I wanted to *be* Superman. I wanted a life that brought good to others, fought the bad guys, rescued the weak, and captured Lois's heart with every adventure.

I never did manage to wear my own cape—other than the day that I graduated from seminary—and I never learned to fly, except as a frequent passenger on a commercial airliner traveling to preach around the country. But I was fortunate enough to capture my own Lois who has faithfully remained by my side for over forty years now. And, as a man—I make it my goal every day to fulfill my responsibilities, as well as to seek the welfare and good of anyone and everyone I can legitimately impact within my realm of influence.

I may not have turned out to be Superman, but it wasn't because I didn't try. Even in those moments, hours, or days when I knew that I did not live up to the powers of my childhood hero—because no man is perfect—something inside of me wouldn't let the idea go. I couldn't escape it. It was my goal.

An important thing to keep in mind about Superman is that he wasn't from Earth. Superman was from another realm that operated by another set of rules. Like the team of football officials, he functioned according to a different book that carried with it a different level of authority. Because of this, he was able to transform the ordinary into the extraordinary while on Earth.

> *Superman was from another realm that operated by another set of rules.*

Likewise, as a kingdom man, you are not from this Earth. Scripture states clearly that you have been seated with Christ in the heavenly realm (Ephesians 2:6). And because of this, you operate with a kingdom set of rules backed by kingdom authority that has the power, when used correctly, to transform your ordinary life into an extraordinary one.

Being a kingdom man is about more than just being a great football player, a great businessman, a successful community leader, or a wealthy individual. Being a kingdom man involves being the hero who aligns himself under the headship and authority of Jesus Christ so he can fully access the power and authority of Jesus Christ to positively influence and impact everything and everyone within his realm.

A kingdom man models himself after the greatest Kingdom Man of all, who over 2000 years ago rescued a world in distress when, rather than call for twelve legions of angels to set Him free from the cross, willingly submitted himself under the orders of His Captain and King—to stand fast for all who would have otherwise been lost.

6

THE REAL MEANING OF HEADSHIP

Not too long ago, my wife, Lois, and I grabbed some time together for a few days. We travelled to Asia Minor and went on an expedition among the ruins where the apostle Paul journeyed. Lois is an avid history fan, and her enthusiasm combined with my own made the trip unforgettable. One of the places that had the most profound impact on me was Corinth. This is because among the excavated ruins of this city was the *bema*. Paul referenced bemas (or judgment seats) a number of times as an earthly illustration of a heavenly location where Jesus Christ will examine each of us according to our faithfulness to God's call on our lives.

This bema rose up as a towering platform, serving in that day as a place for political speeches, public appearances by officials, as well as the location where athletic winners were crowned with their laurels. In Paul's illustration, the bema was a place to receive a reward based entirely on a performance.[1]

While Paul refers to the bema seat as a place to receive your reward for how you lived as a Christian, though, what many men fail to realize is that it is also a place to realize what you may have lost because of how you did not live out your Christian life. (Both 2 Corinthians 5:10 and Romans 14:10–12 mention standing before the judgment seat.) What is revealed at the bema is whether you were a kingdom man on earth, properly aligned under Jesus Christ, or whether you were an earthly man. How well you lived in light of advancing God's cause in history will determine the rights and privileges granted to you during the one-thousand-year kingdom reign of Christ.

While we live in a nation replete with biblical teaching in church buildings located on nearly every street corner as well as carried over the radio and television waves, what concerns me is the number of individuals who do not live in light of the bema. This concerns me because if we overlook how long, real, tangible, and authentic this thousand-year kingdom reign of Christ will be—which we, as believers, will take part in—we may stand upon the bema one day only to weep at the loss we will experience because our life did not focus on God's kingdom. This is a thousand years, men. That's a long time no matter how you slice it. Now is the time to position yourself either as a street sweeper or the ruler over towns, cities, and nations based on how you align yourself with Christ's headship and His kingdom agenda.

The primary principle upon which your destiny forms as a kingdom man, both now and in the future, involves the concept of headship—alignment. Paul introduced this truth into the setting of a chaotic Corinthian church located directly in the heart of this most licentious city of the first century.

> *In Corinth, everything was out of order. In fact, it was a free-for-all.*

If you have ever read 1 Corinthians, you know that chapter after chapter simply covers problem after problem. In Corinth, everything was out of order. In fact, it was a free-for-all, resulting in unprecedented amounts of division, pain, and confusion within the church. It was unprecedented for then; however, it is often seen as normal for now. Yet when Paul addressed the Corinthian church, he had to deal with the influx of chaos by taking them back to the beginning. Because it was such a mess, he had to take them back to the fundamentals.

Paul's wording is so foundational that it reminds me of the legendary football coach Vince Lombardi on the day he addressed his then-struggling Green Bay Packers. The scene is iconic in all of our minds, I'm sure. With a football in hand, Lombardi turned to face the roomful of professional athletes half his age and twice his size and said, "Gentlemen, this is a football."[2]

Lombardi had just made the simplest statement in football history.

Lombardi's point was that before the players went any further, they must master the basics first. The same holds true with being a kingdom man. Men, before we dig deeper into the areas of authority, dominion, and courageous ruling, Paul said that we must start with the basics of alignment and headship. There is no going deeper without owning this first, since all else builds upon it. Paul wrote in 1 Corinthians 11, "Be imitators of me, just as I also am of Christ. . . . I want you to understand that Christ is the head of every man, and the man is the head of a woman, and God is the head of Christ" (1,3).

You can't get much more basic than that. Christ is the head of every man.

The man is the head of *a* woman.

And God is the head of Christ.

Anyone who knows me well knows that I approach things from the end and work my way backward. I start at the end goal, or the bottom line, and then move backward to see how it was either accomplished or ought to be accomplished. So, now that you know that, it shouldn't surprise you that I want to unpack these verses starting at the end.

God Is the Head of Christ

For starters, let's look at the whole idea of the *head*. The concept of headship extends much further than just a delineation of authority. The idea of headship includes covering, provision, protection, guidance, and responsibility. These characteristics define Christ's relationship with the church as the head of the church. In Ephesians 5:25–33, we read that a man is to emulate Christ in his marriage as head.

The Greek word Paul used for head in this verse is *kephale*,[3] which denotes the physical head on top of a human being or animal. As you are well aware, the head is the central location for four of the five bodily senses. It does much more than make a final decision in anything. In fact, when King Herod's wife, Herodias, wanted to stop John the Baptist's criticism concerning her marriage to Herod, she only had to ask her husband to serve John's head on a platter to her. Without a head, John the Baptist couldn't do anything at all. The head is critical to the overall functioning of what is under its influence—whether that be a physical body in a literal sense, or a particular person or group in a metaphorical sense.

Headship isn't about essence or being; it is about function. We know that Christ's ontological being is the same essence as God, but when it came to functioning on Earth, Jesus came under God to carry out the divine plan. Theology also clearly tells us that Jesus is equal to God. Headship doesn't determine or reflect a lack of equality. In fact, Jesus himself states clearly that He "and the

Father are one" (John 10:30). Likewise, headship doesn't deny oneness. Rather, headship defines function.

If headship wasn't about function, then the crucifixion would have never happened. Jesus would have never been buried. He would have never been resurrected. And as a result, we would have never had redemption, justification, sanctification, or been able to look forward to glorification. Because in the garden, as sweat mixed with blood and dripped off of His body, Jesus clearly vocalized that, if at all possible, He didn't want to go through with the plan set before Him—the Cross. Yet because Jesus understood and lived out the principles of headship, He yielded His reticence to God's will saying, "Father, if You are willing, remove this cup from Me; yet not My will, but Yours be done" (Luke 22:42).

If ever there was an illustration of the crucial nature and accomplishment of biblical headship, Calvary was it. Jesus was able to function in alignment at Calvary, in the heat of the battle, because He held an accurate understanding and practice of it prior to Calvary. Elsewhere in John 6:38, He said, "For I have come down from heaven, not to do My own will, but the will of Him who sent Me." Jesus operated with the correct mind-set. Because of Christ's submission to the headship over Him, then you and I, and anyone who puts his trust in Him for salvation, will now have a drastically different eternity than we would have had if Christ had chosen to do His own thing instead. I don't know about you, but I am grateful for headship.

The Man Is the Head of a Woman

Before we move onto the next section of the verse that pertains directly to a man's relationship to Christ, I want to touch on the often controversial middle section of 1 Corinthians 11:3 where we read that "the man is the head of a woman." Since this is a book for men, I am not going to go into all of the details of the submission of a woman right here.[4] And men, if you are single, take notes on this section so you will have the right understanding when you get married. But what I do want to point out is that the Scripture clearly states that the man is the head of *a* woman, not the head of *all* women. This is not a blanket ticket for male domination; rather this is a hierarchical structure for the home (if a woman is married), and for the church (if a woman is single and no longer under her father's authority).[5]

Likewise, I want to note that this does not mean that a man has absolute authority over a woman. He has authority over a woman only as long as it is consistent with the Word of God. For example, a man cannot tell his wife to rob a bank then hold her guilty for not submitting if she doesn't do it. The man's authority, as we are about to see, must directly be placed under the authority of Jesus Christ for it to be legitimate, which is why Paul says a woman is to be subject to her husband "as to the Lord" (Ephesians 5:22).

I want to mention something else that has to do with one of the most beautiful things about women. You may know what I am talking about before I even get there. And that is that women were designed to respond. Innate within a woman lies a responsive mechanism enabling her to uniquely fulfill her divine destiny in completing a man and being completed by a man.

Now, because of how some women were raised, perhaps in an atmosphere of abuse or in a strong matriarchal home, they may not recognize or exhibit this trait, but women have been created to receive and respond. It is built into how God programmed them. It is even built into them biologically as to how they have been anatomically designed. Don't think too long on that one—I want you to stay with me. Women have been created to receive and respond physiologically, emotionally, and spiritually.

But what you need to know about a woman is that just as much as she can receive and respond positively, she can also receive and respond negatively. If the wrong things are said or done to her, she may react in a way that reflects what is being done to her. Because of that, you could end up with nagging or a rebellious heart. Or, if she lacks attention or protection, then she will receive that and respond by doing everything in her power to protect or provide for herself, as well as position herself in a way so she won't run the risk of being let down again. All she is doing is giving you the feedback based on what you are giving to her. She is a mirror reflecting to you the impact and influence that you, or other males, have had on her.

If you want a summer wife, men, then don't bring home winter weather.

If you want a summer wife, men, then don't bring home winter weather. But if you have a winter wife, men, then it is time to bring out the sun. Women have been created to receive and respond; therefore, you regulate much of the temperature in your home. Of course, there may be extenuating factors out of your control, but for the most part, men simply are not recognizing or maximizing the power of their influence in the home.

Keep in mind, though, that this can take some time. Depending upon how long biblical manhood has been absent in a woman's life, that may be how long it takes for her to receive and respond because she needs to be sure biblical manhood is real when it does show up. She is not going to expose herself in a vulnerable manner just because you say that you heard a sermon, read a book, went to a conference, or had a great morning devotion. Neither is she going to be vulnerable if she thinks that you are just talking nicely so you can turn up the heat in the bedroom. For a woman to receive and respond by willingly placing herself under the functional headship of a man, she wants to know that you are a kingdom man and that you are under the headship of Christ.

This concept is all about the covering. When she knows that you are covered by God, she will respond to your covering her. She will rest. When she hears you say, "I've got it," and then she sees that backed up by your actions, she will follow you.

When you are a kingdom man, when she hears you say, "I've got it," when you lead with compassion, consistency, and wisdom, when you involve her in every significant decision, and when you value her input and desires, you will discover that your relationship with her will go to a level you never dreamed possible. For a man to be "over a woman," he must take seriously his responsibility for her well-being. He must cover her in such a way that she is free to respond well.

Christ Is the Head of Every Man

As I counseled a husband and his wife, I asked the man if he was going to do what he had just agreed God's Word said that he should do.

He answered, "I'm not sure."

So I took a moment to clarify that he believed that what God had said was true. He said that he did. Then I asked him again if he was going to do it. He still didn't think that he would. I said, "Suppose your wife told you that she loved you but that she wasn't going to do what you wanted her to do?" He didn't like that at all. But headship and covering work both ways. A man covers a woman because Christ covers a man. To hold a woman accountable to something that you yourself are not willing to do is a double standard, and it is one of the major reasons that cause the breakdown of the family.

If a man is expecting a woman to be answerable to him, she should see him modeling that same principle by being answerable to God's headship as well. In my years of counseling, I more often than not come across men who expect everyone else to answer to them without them having to answer to anyone. What many men do is disrespect the headship of Christ, but expect the woman living with him to respect his headship over her.

God rules His world representatively. While He is the ultimate Ruler and sovereign over all, God has historically ruled through representatives such as judges, prophets, kings, and, in the age of the new covenant, He established His rule in the church through the elders and leaders (see 1 Timothy 3 and Titus 1). Yet when headship is not aligned properly, His presence, power, and authority in his representatives are compromised or lost.

Since Paul was writing to the church, we know that he was talking about Christian men in particular when he wrote that, "Christ is the head of every man" (Corinthians 11:3). Every Christian man, therefore, has a head in the same way that Jesus, the son of God, had Someone over Him who covered, provided for, and guided, and to whom He was accountable. No Christian man is autonomous. Every Christian man, whether single or married, is answerable to Jesus Christ. When a man learns to submit his maleness to the lordship of Jesus Christ, he is living out the basic principles of kingdom manhood.

But the question I often hear when I lead a monthly men's Bible study or counsel married couples is this: How do we live this out in everyday life where we see, feel, hear, touch and smell? Jesus Christ, after all, isn't standing right there in front of us. Often, in fact, a woman will voice her concern in counseling that she is supposed to be functionally under the man, but he is under Christ, which leaves room for no earthly accountability.

Yet a further look at Scripture reveals a significant amount of accountability for men, because God instituted His church to be the human manifestation of the rule of Christ. An incomplete ecclesiological understanding in many of our churches today has led to a dearth in accountability for men in the body of Christ.

I'm going to write more about the comprehensive nature of the church, as well as a man's role in it and through it during a later chapter, but I want to briefly look at the church as the visible expression of Christ's rule on Earth now in relationship to headship. Colossians 1:18 says, "He [Jesus Christ] is also head of the body, the church; and He is the beginning, the firstborn from the dead, so that He Himself will come to have first place in everything."

Paul wrote in Ephesians 1:22–23, "And He put all things in subjection under His feet, and gave Him as head over all things to the church, which is His body, the fullness of Him who fills all in all." The church, established as a governing body in subjection to Christ, has been designed to uniquely carry out the role of manifesting God's rule on earth.[6] A man who is not under the leadership and guidance of the local church is not living under the headship of Christ since the church is the body and fullness of Christ. Keep in mind that filling a suit on Sunday does not constitute being under the leadership and guidance of the church.

> *The biblical kingdom-minded church was a central location involved in multiple aspects of daily life.*

The biblical kingdom-minded church was a central location involved in multiple aspects of daily life.

The *ekklésia*, which is translated into the contemporary word *church*, essentially involved a group of citizens convened in a specific location for the purposes of deliberation as well as for establishing or communicating governing measures. As part of the *ekklésia* in Greek societies, a man belonged to a group of individuals who issued and carried out legislation on behalf of the Greek population. It was more than just a place to hear great singing and inspirational thoughts. It was a formal location designed for establishing a formal code for societal matters.[7]

A man's involvement with the church, the *ekklésia*, should reach beyond the two hours on a Sunday. His involvement is where he is to receive guidance and accountability, as well as where he is to participate in establishing the overarching strategy for affecting the citizens around him.

Being involved at a greater level does not mean, however, that a man shouldn't lead his wife or family in devotions or that he shouldn't take it upon himself to pray, study God's Word and grow as a follower of Christ. But the church is to function as a place of direction to assist a man in living as a kingdom man. In fact, the church is to be the place where a man gathers the truths of God's Word to take back home to his family to teach them in more detail.

The church is also to serve as a place where those who have received training in studying God's Word are available to answer questions that men may have as they seek to teach and disciple the members of their home. Yet far too frequently it seems that it is the women who are bringing the questions to the pastors and church leaders instead. Men, this is your job. If your wife or children have a question, it is your responsibility to hunt it down and provide an answer for them. If your wife is referencing your pastor's name more than yours during the week, you are not adequately satisfying your role as spiritual head in your home. You are your wife's pastor.

A major component of being a pastor comes in thinking about what the person or people under your care need to grow spiritually. As your wife's pastor, you need to intentionally consider what your wife needs to mature in her walk with Christ. And then you need to take steps to provide those things for her.

The role of the pastor involves shepherding, consistent discipleship, mediation, counseling (lending an empathetic and wise ear), and oversight. How many people would attend a church where the pastor showed up to preach once every three or four months? Not many. Just as a pastor in a church needs to take his role and responsibilities seriously, as the pastor in your home, you need to create an environment where your wife looks to you for spiritual leadership and covering.

The Role of the Church

One of my growing concerns in our culture is that in our shift toward a more convenience-store church mentality, we are drifting dangerously away from the significant role the church is to play in the life of every believer. Within a fully operational church—depending on the depth of the situation—the guidance and assistance that men need to maximize their biblical manhood come in many forms. For some men, the church serves as a place of teaching, personal ministry, fellowship, and encouragement. For other men, personal discipleship needs may be so high that they need deeper accountability in addition to everything else. When men begin to function in their homes, accountable to the guidance and direction of a leader in the church, things change. I have personally seen men transform their marriages that they had originally thought were headed straight to court. The transformations occurred when they willingly placed themselves under the guidance and counsel of a pastor, associate pastor, or church leader.

As I mentioned earlier, women are made to respond to how a man handles himself and relates to her. Men, when you lead well, you don't have to push, pull, demand, or berate a woman to have her fulfill her role in your family. When you lead well, and when she sees the security that she has in knowing that she can respond to your headship because you submit to Christ's headship, she will respond under you if she has any spiritual sensitivity at all. When you are willing to temporarily replace sexual intimacy with spiritual intimacy as Paul instructed in 1 Corinthians 7:5, your wife will not only see your seriousness and respect it, but heaven will also see it and respond.

> *You should not be surprised if a woman is not following your lead if you are not following Christ's lead.*

The problem in marriages today isn't that we have too many women who don't want to submit. The problem is that we have too many men who don't want to submit—to the headship of Jesus Christ. You should not be surprised if a woman is not following your lead if you are not following Christ's lead. If you are not openly and actively following Christ's lead, you cannot complain when your wife is not following you.

Sin in your life—whether from sins of omission or sins of commission—will remove you from a correct alignment under God. Righteousness—which is not perfection but an honest and regular confession of sin, turning from sin, and intentionally seeking to do and think what is right according to God's truth—will keep you in alignment under Him.

If you find that you are out of alignment with God, you need to get back in it as quickly as possible through confession and repentance. If you are not a Christian, then you are not aligned with God. To align yourself under Him, I want to encourage you to place your trust in Jesus Christ as your personal Savior for the forgiveness of your sins based on His substitutionary* death on the cross and His resurrection from the dead. And, after you do so, I want to be the first to welcome you as a brother in Christ.

---

* This means Jesus died in your place, as a substitute.

Yet if you are a Christian but not following God's kingdom plan—not aligned under Him—I want to encourage you to make the personal commitment to align every area of your life so that it operates under the headship of Jesus Christ. When you are aligned under Him, those within your realm—as well as yourself—will be blessed. In theology, we discover something powerful called the principle of representation. I briefly touched on representation when I mentioned that Adam had been created as a prototype for all humankind and Jesus was the new prototype for kingdom men. These prototypes are also referred to in Scripture as the *first* and *last* Adam (1 Corinthians 15:45). The first Adam ushered in sin and its destruction, while the last Adam brought us eternal life.

Yet what is essential to understanding and applying the truths of headship in your life is that in the principle of representation, the person who is placed over you can act for you. So depending on who is—or is not—over you will determine many things in your life. When you live as a kingdom man under the headship of Jesus Christ, you receive the benefits of His representation before God in heaven. You receive what He receives in "proxy," and those under you will receive it too.

Later, when we look at my all-time favorite passage of Scripture, Psalm 128, I'll tell you more about the blessings you receive when you are under your representative headship, Jesus Christ. But don't just take my word for it, do it, and experience the blessing of headship yourself.

PART II

THE FOUNDATION OF A KINGDOM MAN

A kingdom man is a man who visibly demonstrates
the comprehensive rule of God underneath the Lordship
of Jesus Christ in every area of his life.

7

DOMINION'S ROAR

The king of the jungle, the lion, has a roar that can be heard up to five miles away. This is especially impressive when you realize that only four animals in the cat family can actually roar at all—the lion, tiger, leopard, and jaguar. These four belong to what is called the *Panthera* group because of their unique two-piece hyoid bone in the throat. No others have it. Yet of the cats that roar, the lion roars the most. The lion roars the longest. And the lion roars the loudest.[1]

A lion's roar has such force that it can actually lift the dust off the ground and create a large whirling circle of dirt in the air in front of him. The roar has been known to cause the metal frames of vehicles to vibrate. And it undoubtedly makes every fine hair on the back of any human's neck stand up at the sound of it, including my own.

I had the opportunity to see lions in the wild on a trip I had taken to South Africa to teach the Kingdom Agenda theology and philosophy to local pastors. Of all of the animals I have ever seen, nothing compares to the majesty of a lion. Even the cheetah that I got to meet up close and personal, and was actually able to stroke, paled in comparison to the lion I saw from a relatively safe distance.

Numbers of men have dedicated countless hours to studying this untamed king. A lion's strength not only fascinates us, but also inspires us. His prowess not only captivates us, but also arouses us. His regality not only allures us, but it also awakens our own.

One of the things that has been studied the most about lions is *why* a lion will roar with such force. Why does a lion sound his roar with the enormous power to extend five miles? Think about it; five miles is no small distance. Five miles is the length of 88 football fields or 283 professional basketball courts, and would take a Ferrari racing at top speeds nearly two minutes to cross it. What is it that propels a lion to roar with such volume to cover that ground? Scientists who study lions have learned over the years that a lion roars for several reasons.

At times a lion roars to warn off intruders, thus fulfilling his role as protector. Other times a lion roars to startle prey, as he gets closer to his final move of taking them down, thus fulfilling his role as provider. Still at other times, a lion roars to reunite scattered pride members, thus fulfilling his role as leader over his own. Another reason that a lion roars, of course, is to attract a female lion in heat, thus fulfilling his role as partner. I probably didn't have to tell you that one.[2]

Of all the reasons that a lion roars, one of them stood out to me as I learned about this magnificent animal on my trip: A lion roars to declare dominion.

Lions are nomadic animals at times because of the need to hunt migratory prey and will roar outside their own territory, or dominion. But they do this infrequently, only in situations of extreme need or intentional aggression. Yet when a lion is in his own territory within his own domain, he will roar multiple times over the course of several hours, usually at night and at the height of pride vulnerability. The lion roars as if to communicate: I have dominion over this land. I have dominion over this pride. I am protecting, providing, leading, and partnering in it. This is my domain.

Not only does the lion's roar send the message of dominion to any other cats that might be looking to enter his land, but it also sends a reassuring sound of security to the members of the lion's pride. What the lion has declared through his roar is that, as ruler, he is responsible. In his dominion, he has the authority to call the shots for whatever goes on within it. If he calls the shots well, he will keep his land and he will keep his pride. In fact, if he calls them well, he will position himself to expand his land and expand his pride.

> *If a lion does not protect his domain, another lion will take what he has.*

Yet if a lion does not protect his domain, another lion will take what he has.

Men, before we go any further, I want to pause to ask you one thing: When was the last time you roared?

I'm not asking when the last time was that you grunted, moaned, or complained about how tough the circumstances are, how bleak the economy looks, how difficult your work situation is, how bad the food tastes, or how your wife or children never seem to listen to you. What I need to know, men, is when was the last time you actually roared? When was the last time that the reassuring strength of your roar was not only heard but also felt by all those within your sphere of influence and under your care? And when was the last time that the force of your roar firmly warded off all those seeking to devour that which is within your domain?

To express your authority within your domain, you must roar. It is not an option. You must protect, provide, lead, and partner well in the areas of your influence. You must also declare your dominion by responsibly exercising your rule within it.

Lost and Found

On a recent walk by the lost and found area at my church in Dallas, Texas, I noticed that the lost and found area seemed to be growing. Either people don't know that they have lost something, or they don't care about whatever it is that has been lost. Most of the things, by the way, in our lost and found are Bibles. These Bibles have sat there for an inordinate amount of time unclaimed, and therefore, unused.

Many men need to visit God's "lost and found" to reclaim the power of the Word of God in their lives so they can exercise it. Far too many men have misplaced their ability to maximize truths found in God's Word. They have misplaced what is absolutely essential to carry out their purpose, the fulfillment of their destiny, and the justification of their significance. As a result, they have difficulty locating, understanding, and fulfilling their right to rule.

The reason so few men are actually going back to reclaim what has been misplaced is either because they don't know that they have lost it, or they don't realize the full value of what they have misplaced—so they don't care that they do not have it. Another reason many men are not reclaiming what is rightfully theirs is because they do not know where to find it. Yet when a man abdicates, or loses, his right to rule, he—often unknowingly—becomes inadvertently ruled by that which is illegitimate. He is ruled by his circumstances, the people around him, his problems, and the challenges he faces. These things rule him because he has lost sight of his own spiritual authority. Rather than being the head, he has become the tail—being wagged every which way by life's storms.

Reclaiming Manhood

My father often reminds me that I loved being a man even before I became one. Whenever I visit, he tells me I always wanted to be a man. He says I would often try to do more than a teenager should. I would try to take on more responsibility than my father was ready to give or ask for more freedom than he was ready to allow.

Invariably, each time I did, he would tell me, "Tony, you're not a man yet."

To which I would always reply, "But I'm almost a man."

I could not wait. Something about being a man fuels me. No other subject that I teach on, preach on, or write about impassions me more. Not because I believe that men have been put here to dominate or control, but because Scripture tells us that we have an enormous responsibility, as well as a right, to rule, or manage, that which has been placed within our dominion. We have the authority to influence and impact everything within our realm. If that doesn't get the blood flowing, I don't know what will. And yet so many men seem to run from dominion or are unaware of their right to exercise it through their rule.

So many men seem to run from dominion or are unaware of their right to exercise it through their rule.

So many of the casualties I have seen in the body of Christ over several decades of ministry have directly resulted—for both the man himself as well as those in connection with him—from a man's not comprehending, grabbing, and living out his God-given authority through his right to rule.

Examining the foundational theology of your spiritual authority as manifested through your right to rule will, in turn, lead you to see how the responsibility of ruling your world plays out. The realm of your responsibility, your dominion, is what I sometimes refer to as your *garden*. Just as Adam was first placed in a garden that God entrusted to him to guard, each of us has our own garden, or domain, that God has placed in our care. You have an area of influence that you have been created to rule. But to understand why you are even given a garden in the first place, you have to comprehend your authority as a kingdom man. Understanding why you get to fully exercise your legitimate, biblical rule is critical in laying the framework for all else.

God Said

When God created the Earth, He demonstrated His genius simply through His Word. Whatever He spoke came into being. Not only did it come into being, but it was also good. In five days, God had created a spectacular Earth with all of the nuances and idiosyncrasies necessary for life to be lived out to its fullest. On the sixth day, God spoke forth His crowning achievement—man. About man, we read that first,

"God said . . ." (Genesis 1:26).

Then, "God created . . ." (Genesis 1:27).

And next, "God blessed . . ." (Genesis 1:28).

Everything related to man in the creation text is directly connected to God and His plan for humankind. God said it, God created it, and God blessed it. Obviously, this is how God intended it. Because we are about to tread into some delicate territory, I don't want you to just take my word for it; take His.

In Genesis 1:26, we read, "Then God said, 'Let Us make man in Our image, according to Our likeness, and let them rule.'"

On the sixth day, God created man in His own image. Both male and female were made in the image of God and given rulership. Yet as is revealed in the theology of headship, men have been called to lead in the exercise of this dominion. Because of this, as well as for the purposes of this book, I have chosen to focus on a male's rulership in this discussion.

The plurality of "Let Us" and "Our image" refers to God's trinitarian nature, indicating the fullness of function found in the creation of man as a reflection of God. Man is an image-bearer of God in that he is responsible to mirror God's character and ways. Instead of the "Made in America" stamp, humankind received the "Made in God's Image" stamp.

Like an automobile built in an assembly plant reflects the nature, purpose, and intention of its creator, humankind has been designed to reflect our Creator. The trucks that come out of the manufacturing plant in Henry Ford's hometown of Dearborn, Michigan, not only carry his name, but also his vision. A truck rolls off of that line having been "Built Ford Tough." Likewise, as men made in the image of God, each of us has been "Built God Tough." So much so that God himself willingly entrusted the managerial rulership on Earth to us.

> *Instead of the "Made in America" stamp, humankind received the "Made in God's Image" stamp.*

Delegates in Charge

When God created man in His image, He delegated the responsibility of caring for and managing His creation. Up until that time, God did all of the work. He separated the water from the land, formed the light, grew the plants, placed the stars in the sky, along with everything else. Up until then, God took care of it all through His spoken Word. Yet, on the sixth day, when God created man, He turned over the running, ruling, and stewardship of the earth to the hands of man. God endowed humankind with both the opportunity and the responsibility for managing what He had made. When God created man, He gave a mandate—the dominion mandate. The dominion mandate, "Let them rule," set man's rulership, or management, in place over what God had created.

That is no small thing, men. Fundamentally, God willingly pulled back His direct control over the earth while simultaneously delegating that direct control to humankind for managing the affairs of history.

Now, before we go any further, I want to make a clear distinction between what the Scripture is talking about and what deism claims. Deism is a belief system that holds that God created the world and then He wound up disappearing somewhere to let it unwind and unravel in the hands of man. That is not what the Scripture says. God has not given up His ownership. Psalm 24:1 unequivocally tells us, "The earth is the LORD's, and all it contains, the world, and those who dwell in it."

God has not turned over absolute ownership of the earth to humankind. But what He has released is the managerial responsibility for ruling it. By turning over the management to man, God has established a process, within certain boundaries, whereby He respects man's decisions—even if those decisions go against Him or even if those decisions are not in the best interest of that which is being managed. God said, "Let them rule . . ." (Genesis 1:26). While God retains absolute sovereign authority and ownership, He has delegated relative authority to man with a sphere of influence, or dominion, for each man.

For example, the bank may own the house you live in, but it is your responsibility to pay a monthly mortgage on the house that you say that you "own," as well as to maintain it, for good or for bad. Now, most people know how great it feels to walk into a house that you just purchased and think to yourself, *I own this house.* But the truth is, in most cases, the bank owns that house.

The bank does not get involved with the everyday duties of running your house—that is your responsibility. Neither does the bank force you to clean your house nor prevent you from having a junky one. That is up to you. Yet, similarly, the bank does not give up ultimate ownership of the house just because you are the one living in it and managing it. If you do not make your payments, you will be the one who faces the consequence of losing that house.

Likewise, a coach does not own the team that he is coaching, but he will often refer to it as "my team" or "my players." While an ultimate owner of the team exists, the coach serves as the managerial ruler of the team. The coach is responsible for how that team functions. This is especially true when a team starts to play poorly. It is usually not the kicker who missed six field goals in a season, or the wide receiver who dropped eight passes in the last four games, or the entire defensive line who couldn't defend the red zone all year long that gets fired. Rather, as a result of all of those things combined, the coach loses his job when his team does not consistently perform well.

The same holds true in the realm where you have been assigned to rule. God is the ultimate owner. He has delegated the responsibility to manage it without having delegated His sovereignty over and within it. Your decisions directly affect the quality of life within your sphere and will have a large bearing on whether your realm of influence increases or decreases with time. God didn't stop Adam from eating the fruit, but He controlled the consequences when Adam did eat the fruit, thus limiting Adam's dominion from what it had originally been ordained to be.

What Satan did in trying to increase his influence on earth has cast a shadow on man's legitimate God-ordained right to rule. Satan's shadow is made up of the stained hues of complacency and insignificance. He has done this in an attempt to handcuff believers from carrying out the responsibilities given to them and to keep them from racing to the "lost and found" to reclaim the authority of their position under God.

David, a man after God's own heart and a king who exercised a great deal of authority, clearly articulated the high level in which God has placed humankind, for good or for bad, showing us the truth of how we are to operate within our sphere of influence. He wrote in Psalm 8:3-6:

> When I consider Your heavens, the work of Your fingers,
> The moon and the stars, which You have ordained;
> What is man that You take thought of him,
> And the son of man that You care for him?
> Yet You have made him a little lower than God,
> And You crown him with glory and majesty!
> You make him to rule over the works of Your hands,
> You have put all things under his feet.

In this passage, David not only praises God for the greatness of His creation, but also for the glory and majesty that He has given to man, as well as man's rule. God has placed a crown on the head of every man, thereby calling him majestic. You are majestic. You are royalty. You are awesome. You are created to be a kingdom man. The enemy does not want you to know that you are all of these things. Satan does not want you to know that you have glory, honor, and dominion, which God himself has given you to live out on earth.

You are a reflection of God, an image-bearer. You get to call the shots, for good or for bad.

As long as Satan can keep you from thinking like royalty, he can keep you from acting like royalty. As long as he can keep you thinking that you are nobody, or that you do not matter and you have no say, he can keep you acting like you are nobody, or that you do not matter and that you have no say. As a result, Satan can keep kingdom men from advancing the kingdom of God as they ought to advance; he lulls those who have been given the legitimate authority to advance into believing that they not only lack significance, but also dominion and authority.

Yet you have been crowned with majesty in God's kingdom. It is up to you to use the rights that come with the majesty that you have been given. While God is the sovereign and absolute King, He has given you an area to rule in His name, by His rules, and in His image as a kingdom man. You are a reflection of God, an image-bearer. You get to call the shots, for good or for bad, and how you call them will determine how chaotic or productive your *garden* becomes. God has placed you in a garden. He has given you the dominion mandate. He has said, "Let them rule . . ."

Take up Your Authority

God has a plan for you. A specific plan. One thing to do to discover that specific plan is to examine your passions, abilities, personality, and experiences, then uncover where those four converge. This will help to reveal the plan God has destined you for.

God has also given you the authority you need to perform that plan well. Maybe you have lost the leverage of that authority somewhere along the way through poor decisions or neglect, or maybe you have even forgotten where that authority is located. But God has a "lost and found" for you to visit to get back what the enemy has taken away.

As a man, you have a charge to keep and a domain to rule. Like the lion's roar that reaches up to five miles declaring his dominion, you have a specific realm God has authorized you to rule. It may not be a physical location as much as it is a sphere of influence. How well you call the shots while ruling your world will determine how much world you get to rule.

One of my favorite aspects of ministry has been serving as the chaplain for the Dallas Cowboys. As you know, before the start of any football game, the home team will swarm together in an electrifying mass of shouts. You have seen them as they form a tight circle of mutual strength, rhythmically moving as if performing some ancient ritual before battle. The cadence of their call penetrates the air as a collective roar. In it, they declare dominion. They declare that this is their house. Another team has arrived to try to invade their house. But their roar reminds them, and everyone else, that not only will the home team defend it, but they will also rule every yard within it.

> *God has given you a domain in which you are to rule. You are responsible not only to defend it but also to expand it.*

You have a house—a realm. God has given you a domain in which you are to rule. You are responsible not only to defend it, but also to expand it.

Kingdom men, it is high time that the world hears you roar.

8

~~

AUTHORIZED TO RULE

God said that you are to rule; He has also given you all that you need to do it. If you memorize only one verse in the Bible in your entire life, memorize 2 Corinthians 9:8. The truth of it will blow your mind: "And God is able to make all grace abound to you, so that always having all sufficiency in everything, you may have an abundance for every good deed."

Anything that you do in God's name for His glory, a good deed, will have His power to do it. It is a guarantee. Look to Him for it. Don't attempt to do things on your own.

When God sent Moses to Egypt to deliver the Israelites from bondage, He empowered Moses to do the enormous task set before him. Leading the Israelites to freedom was in Moses' dominion. It was in the sphere of influence, or the garden, where God had placed him. God had told him to go. And when He told him, He said, "See, I make you *as* God to Pharaoh, and your brother Aaron shall be your prophet. You shall speak all that I command you, and your brother Aaron shall speak to Pharaoh that he let the sons of Israel go out of his land" (Exodus 7:1-2).

God told Moses that He was going to make him "as God to Pharaoh" even though Pharaoh was the one on earth whom everyone thought was running the show. Everyone thought that Pharaoh held the control, that Pharaoh roared the loudest and the longest, and that Pharaoh called the shots. Yet God trumps everyone, and when God sends someone into the domain that He has declared for him to rule, God empowers that person to do just that. God didn't make Moses *be* God, but He made Moses "*as* God to Pharaoh"—meaning God designated

Moses as His chosen representative to exercise delegated authority, even over someone who seemingly held more earthly authority over Moses.

It doesn't matter what opposition you face as a man—it doesn't matter how big the pharaohs are. If you are in the garden—the domain—where God has placed you, He will give you the power to rule with authority to advance His kingdom.

Accept the Role

Keep in mind, though, that God won't force you to rule, just like He didn't force Moses to confront Pharaoh. That is up to you. Moses could have walked away and said, "You know what, God, that sounds good, and that sounds all tough, and that is a great locker room speech, but have you seen Pharaoh? Do you have any idea how many men he has at his disposal? I appreciate the vote of confidence, God, but You are just not being realistic."

Moses could have said all of that and left. Moses could have abdicated his right to rule out of fear or just plain complacency. If he had, we might be reading about someone else in the Bible whom God used to set His people free. Instead, Moses eventually said, "I've got it."

> *Moses could have abdicated his right to rule out of fear or just plain complacency.*

This is similar to what David said when he faced his own "Pharaoh." Remember that the anatomy of David's "Pharaoh" included a frame that towered at nine feet nine inches tall. Just to give you an idea of how tall that is, if that man were standing next to an NBA basketball hoop set at regulation height, the top of his head would be just under the rim. If he stood on his toes, he would be taller than the rim. The name that this mammoth specimen went by was Goliath from Gath. I'm sure he drooled when he spoke.

What is important to understand about this giant named Goliath was that he likely hailed from a group of people who traced their roots beyond this planet. We are first introduced to them in the book of Genesis: "The sons of God came in to the daughters of men, and they bore *children* to them. Those were the *mighty men*" (Genesis 6:4, emphasis added). Theirs is an epic story rivaling any award-winning blockbuster of our day. They were a mixed breed of fallen angels called the Nephilim, or giants, and while most were annihilated in the flood, remnants could be found afterward. Here are three of those fit for the big screen:

> There was war at Gath again, where there was a man of *great* stature who had six fingers on each hand and six toes on each foot, twenty-four in number; and he also had been born to the giant. (2 Samuel 21:20).

> (For only Og king of Bashan was left of the remnant of the Rephaim [giants]. Behold, his bedstead was an iron bedstead; it is in Rabbah of the sons of Ammon. Its length was nine cubits and its width four cubits by ordinary cubit.) (Deuteronomy 3:11)

> All the people . . . are men of *great size*. There also we saw the Nephilim (the sons of Anak are part of the Nephilim); and we became like grasshoppers in our own sight, and so we were in their sight. (Numbers 13:32–33)

It is highly probable that Goliath came from this rare species, one of a dying breed of giants whose reputation was enough to keep an enemy at bay and whose looming presence dominated the landscape.

Yet when David approached Goliath, he saw much more than a giant. At half Goliath's size, David only had to look straight ahead to be reminded of a whole lot more about this man, because David's vantage point reminded him that Goliath had not been circumcised.

The Right Angle

Perspective is never just what you see. Perspective is how you view what you see. Perspective is a key tool in the hands of a kingdom man if he is going to successfully rule with authority over the domain God has given him. The Israelites saw the same giant that David saw; they just didn't see the giant the same way. The Israelites looked at his size, strength, and body structure. David looked straight ahead at a very critical reality: *Goliath had not been circumcised.* "Then David spoke to the men who were standing by him, saying, 'What will be done for the man who kills this Philistine and takes away the reproach from Israel? For who is this uncircumcised Philistine, that he should taunt the armies of the living God?" (1 Samuel 17:26).

Everyone else had seen how large the giant loomed, but David saw something more important. The giant hadn't been to the doctor. No circumcision only could mean one thing—no covering. Circumcision was a ritual of the covenant between God and His people. All males in Israel were circumcised on the eighth day to signify that they belonged to this covenant and to position themselves under its provision, power, and covering.

> *The Israelites saw the same giant that David saw; they just didn't see the giant the same way.*

To be circumcised meant that you belonged to the family of God. To be uncircumcised meant that God was not on your side—there was no divine covering. You were a pagan. Now, you may be a big and intimidating pagan, but you were still just a pagan. It is as simple, or as difficult, as that. I say it is as simple because it is an obvious truth. But it is also as difficult because so many men in the Israelite army missed it. They looked up at the towering brute standing before them and cowered in fear. David didn't look up. He looked straight ahead and said, "I've got it because God's got it. That man has not been cut." As a result, David accessed God's authority to defeat a giant twice his size.

Men, never let the size of your giant determine the size of your God.

And Your Decision. . .

Many men have, unfortunately, given away their spiritual authority because they lack a kingdom perspective. Satan didn't even have to battle them for it. They simply examined the situation, saw the size of the challenge, or looked at their own inadequacies, and gave up. In so doing, authority over that situation at work, that situation in the home, that problem, that addiction, that ambition, or that vision was handed over to Satan.

Authority to rule is no small thing, and it should be guarded and managed fiercely. In fact, your right to rule is so integral to life that God himself will regularly wait on your decision before He does what He is going to do. Even though the battle was the Lord's, David still had to sling the stone. When God turned over the managerial authority to rule on earth, He placed himself in a position where He at times willingly waits on man. "The Lord is not slow about His promise, as some count slowness, but is patient toward you, not wishing for any to perish but for all to come to repentance" (2 Peter 3:9). God exercises patience, waiting for an action by man before He carries out His promise.

Remember what happened when Abraham was asked to sacrifice his son, Isaac, on the altar in Genesis 22. The substitute sacrificial ram was in the bush all along, but the angel did not reveal the ram to Abraham until Abraham raised the knife in obedience to God's command to sacrifice his son.

Likewise when Abraham had been promised this same son decades earlier when he did not yet have a son, Abraham chose to rule according to his own wisdom by having a child with his handmaiden, Hagar, instead of his wife, Sarai. God did not step in to intervene in Abraham's rule. He allowed Abraham's rule, for good or for bad. Yet because of it, He delayed the onset of the promised heir through Sarai some twenty-five years.

God never forces you to rule your world or manage the domain that He has given you. But He has provided you with everything that is necessary to maximize your own life and everyone else's life within your sphere of influence. You are not merely a bunch of dirt thrown together to exist for a few decades and then die. But far too many men trudge through life with that mentality—waking up to the same breakfast every morning, heading to the same job every day, taking the same lunch break, driving home to watch the same television programs, and then sleeping in the same bed—only to wake up the next morning to do it all over again without any passion, zeal, or purpose to see God's kingdom advance through ruling well. Remember, what you do on earth pays forward into how you will be rewarded in eternity. What you do matters. Not just to others. It matters to you.

What you do doesn't matter only if you are the CEO of a Fortune 500 company or a taxi driver—what you do matters whatever your career may be. God's kingdom encompasses all. Just as there are no unnecessary players on a football team, there are no less valuable positions in God's kingdom.

God has turned over the operation and carrying out of His plan, within prescribed boundaries, to you. Just like a football field has sidelines that are established as physical boundaries within which a coach must call his plays, God has established boundaries around His creation. Within those boundaries, He has given you the freedom to call the plays. A tennis player isn't free to play tennis if there is no baseline. A baseball player isn't free to play baseball if there is no foul line. There are always boundaries in athletics for the game to be maximized. This is also why God has given boundaries in His Word, to create the opportunity to take full advantage of dominion within them. Primarily those boundaries involve His will through the two greatest commandments: loving God and loving others.

What's the Wait?

Some evangelicals today have declared that we can't get in the game but instead need to wait on God to decide to do everything. So they end up doing nothing for the kingdom, nothing eternally productive at all. Because while they are busy waiting on God, He is waiting on them.

The Bible does tell us that at times we are to "Wait for the LORD; Be strong and let your heart take courage; Yes, wait for the LORD" (Psalm 27:14). But to wait on the Lord does not mean to sit down and do nothing. To wait on the Lord for a job does not mean that you sit at home all day and wait for the phone to ring. If that is all you do, you will be waiting on a job for a very long time. If you need a job, and even if you believe God has promised to supply you with a job, you still need to get up, get dressed, brush your teeth, put on your deodorant, and go looking for a job.

We read about this in Matthew 6:26, where it says, "Look at the birds of the air, that they do not sow, nor reap nor gather into barns, and *yet* your heavenly Father feeds them." A bird does not create or provide its own food, but it still has to do something to get the food that has been provided for it. A bird can't just sit on a branch with its beak wide open waiting for God to drop a worm down from heaven. Any bird that does will not last on that branch for very long before it dies of starvation and falls off.

Rather, the bird needs to look for a worm, or a bug, or a seed that God has provided. To wait on the Lord does not mean not taking responsibility. It simply means not going outside of God's rule as you actively exercise authority. It means waiting on God's methods, God's direction, and God's provision to accomplish what God has guided you to do or said that He will do.

Waiting on God does not mean doing nothing—unless there is nothing to do. Waiting on God means not going outside God's prescribed revelation to get something done. God is waiting on you to take the step of faith or the plan of action that He has given to you. You are waiting on God's means, God's guidance, or God's methods to do it. Often that will require your taking action in faith first. I say "in faith" because frequently God's spiritual means do not always reflect the physical realities we see.

To wait on the Lord does not mean to sit down and do nothing.

When I was much younger, in seminary working on my doctorate and planting a church as a new preacher, money was very tight. There were six of us in the home trying to make it on a meager salary coupled with the high expenses of tuition. I remember one time in particular when my car started making a lot of noise. In fact, it was making so much noise that Lois could tell long before I ever got home that I was close to getting home. At the time, all I had was $50 left for the month. But that $50 had already been designated as God's money. It was our tithe.

When Sunday came around, I had to make a decision. Was I going to trust God's Word and let my actions reflect my faith? Or was I going to keep a portion or all of the money to fix my car? The offering plate came by, and all of my $50 went in it.

A couple of days later, my car did more than just make some noise. Smoke started pouring out of the hood. After I pulled over and got out of the car, the smoke turned into flames and the front of my car burned up. So there I was standing next to my car on fire!

Remembering my faith in giving God His money, I admit that I started to feel disappointed. I had honored God according to how He had instructed me in His Word, and this was how He came through for me?

Sure, I had insurance on the car to fix it, but I had a towing fee to pay as well as a $200 deductible to pay first, which might as well have been a $20,000 deductible because I had nothing. However, when I got to the repair shop, they had already started working on the car. I rushed over to the mechanic and told him to stop. "I don't have the money for the deductible," I said, "You need to stop working on it because I can't pay you."

That is when he asked me if I had looked at the fine print of my insurance policy that I had given him earlier.

"No, I haven't," I replied, wondering how that would matter at all since two hundred dollars is two hundred dollars.

"Well, the fine print on your policy says that you don't have to pay the deductible if your car catches on fire."

God had waited—in spite of my need—until I had given Him what He had asked of me, my $50, before meeting my need as He had promised.

Men, God has given us a life to live, a sphere of influence in which to align our choices and decisions in such a way to impact others. But often, He will wait to see what we do before revealing what He does because "Without faith it is impossible to please *Him*, for he who comes to God must believe that He is and *that* He is a rewarder of those who seek Him" (Hebrews 11:6).

> *"He who comes to God must believe that He is and that He is a rewarder of those who seek Him."*

Psalm 115:16 tells us the fullness of the rule that has been entrusted to us: "The heavens are the heavens of the LORD, but the earth He has given to the sons of men." We were created to manage this third rock from the sun, for good or for bad. It has been given to the sons of men. That is a fairly large gift, by the way. And with any fairly large gift comes an equally large amount of responsibility. Yet any man who has ever held a leadership position knows clearly that responsibility without authority is ultimately no responsibility at all. God has not only given you responsibility, men, when He said, "Let them rule," but He has also given you the authority to exercise your rule within your domain with your personal responsibility within His own sovereign boundaries.

This explains why most of the time when God wanted to do something on Earth, as recorded in Scripture, He found a person through whom to do it. He didn't just come down and do it himself. He created an Adam, found a Noah, located an Abraham, sought out a Moses, raised up a judge, identified a prophet, chose a king, and when stuff got really bad, He became a man. God has designed His kingdom to function in such a way that humankind serves as His management team. God has a flowchart, and you are on it—directly over your domain, your sphere of influence. He has positioned you on earth for dominion to bring about the fulfillment of His kingdom plan.

God himself has given you authority, within boundaries, to operate on His behalf in history. You are God's go-between, reaching up to touch heaven and transform Earth.

God Created

As we saw earlier in the book of Psalms, man has been made, "a little lower than God." That's a big difference from what the world tries to tell you in saying that you have been made a little higher than the apes. Big difference.

The image of God in man manifests itself in both an ontological and a functional reality. The ontological reflection of God is found in the spiritual nature. God is spirit, and Scripture tells us that because God is spirit, we must worship Him "in spirit and truth" (John 4:24). When God created man, it says that He "breathed into his nostrils the breath of life; and man became a living being" (Genesis 2:7). Adam became a living soul when the immaterial spirit was placed within him.

Yet not only does your image as a man reflect God ontologically, but it also reflects Him functionally. Because man has been created in God's image, man's rulership must reflect God's rulership for man's to be successful. In this way, man's physical reality is to mirror God's spiritual reality when he rules according to God's prescribed framework.

A man who is spiritually connected to God carries out the rule of God through combining the spiritual with the physical reality of function. We were created as holistic beings, reflecting God's image. However, what Satan has been successful at doing is getting us to separate our ontological reality from our functional reality, so we are spiritual on Sunday, but we approach life independently from God through the physical, tangible realities Monday through Saturday. What this has caused is a form of spiritual schizophrenia in the body of Christ, limiting man's advancement of the kingdom of God.

For a man's rulership to accomplish all that God intends for it to do, it must come under God's overarching rule while simultaneously reflecting God's image. Rulership is never to be apart from the image. What we frequently experience in our culture is men who want to rule without the image. When men try to carry out their rule without integrating the spiritual aspect into the physical rulership, God ends up cast aside while consequences mount up.

A Kingdom Man Rules with Help

An essential component of integrating the spiritual aspect into the physical ruler-ship is in possessing an accurate understanding of the divinely intended function between a man and a woman. Much of the confusion that surrounds marriages today stems from an inaccurate view of the nature of this relationship. When people read that God said it was not good for Adam to be alone, they frequently equate that to implying that God was assuaging Adam's loneliness through creat-ing a woman. They equate it essentially and simply to companionship.

Yet if it were only companionship that was missing, we would more likely be reading that Adam was the one saying it was not good for him to be alone. Rather, it was God who made the statement. Adam didn't mention it at all. As well, the specific Hebrew words used to describe the woman as a helper made specifically for Adam do not refer in any form or manner to someone who has been designed just to remove loneliness. Rather, only one clear reason exists for God to say, " 'I will make him a helper suitable for him" (Genesis 2:18), and that is because Adam obviously needed the help.

While Adam had been created perfectly, he had also been created incomplete. God created Adam in such a way that the task of carrying out dominion could not sufficiently be done without assistance. Adam alone could not pull off God's design for his life. To advance into an even greater level of dominion, Adam needed help.

This is not to negate the value of companionship or that Eve met a need for companionship, but companionship was not God's primary concern when He created a woman. God's concern was in empowering the man and, as a result, empowering both to exercise rule.

To put it another way, men, strategically pursuing your calling—or your destiny—precedes your sexuality. Having someone by your side who can help you achieve what God has determined for you takes priority over how steamy things are in the bedroom. Likewise, having assistance to reach your full potential is more important than how pretty someone is. I'm not saying that God didn't throw in some fun along the way for you to have with her and for her to have with you, but His purpose stretches far beyond companionship or gaining a trophy for a wife. Yet because many men have made the latter the goal at the expense of the former, either because of an inaccurate understanding of what they should be looking for in a companion or short-sighted values, they have not maximized the potential of the marital covenantal union.

The Hebrew words that have been translated into *helper suitable for him* in the passage we just looked at are important to examine because they are a lot more powerful than what we often give them credit. These words are *ezer*[1] and *kenegdo*.[2] The word *ezer* occurs twenty-one times in the Old Testament, with only two of those times referring to a woman. The remaining usages refer specifically to help coming directly from God in a superior form. For example,

"There is none like the God of Jeshurun, Who rides the heavens to your help [*ezer*]." (Deuteronomy 33:26)

Our soul waits for the LORD; He is our help [*ezer*] and our shield. (Psalm 33:20)

But I am afflicted and needy; Hasten to me, O God! You are my help [*ezer*]. (Psalm 70:5)

Our help [ezer] is in the name of the LORD. (Psalm 124:8)

To distinguish *ezer* from every other use in the Old Testament, which referred to a stronger help brought about by God, the word *kenegdo* was added, which comes from *neged* meaning in front of or in sight of. This is also translated to mean a completion of or a counterpart to, as in a mate.[3] Men, if your view of the woman you have married—or if you are single, the woman you will marry—is simply someone who cooks, cleans your house, wipes noses, and drives the kids to soccer practice, you have not just missed the spiritual component of the nature of a relationship between a man and a woman, you have misused that relationship— to your own detriment. If all you want is someone to do your chores, then I suggest you hire a maid. Because Eve was created for much more than that. Eve was created to provide, what a contextual understanding of the multiple uses of *ezer* informs us is, a *strong help* in the position of *counterpart.* Advancing in your destiny is a collaborative effort, men, if you want to advance well.

Any man who does not view his mate and look to her skills, insight, intellect, training, and giftedness is a foolish man. Any man who does not actively encourage her and provide a way for her to sharpen her skills, intellect, and training is an equally foolish man. Too many men, particularly in American Christian culture, waste what God has created within the woman they have married, frequently because they do not respect her differences—particularly her emotions. A man will often dismiss the importance of a woman's emotions while it is precisely her emotions that can balance his logic. God has uniquely designed the female brain to pick up on more perceptions and intuition than the male brain. While that is not always the case, it is often the case. Therefore, if you do not value her understanding of an issue, you will be making a decision without the complete picture and without all of the information—because she completes you as a counterpart to you.

> *To undervalue the woman in your life is one of the gravest mistakes you could ever make.*

The less a woman feels appreciated, needed, and valued as equal with you, the less responsive she will be to following your functional lead as the head in your home. To undervalue the woman in your life is one of the gravest mistakes you could ever make. In fact, Peter makes it inextricably clear that a failure to honor her as a fellow heir will actually keep God from responding to your prayers (1 Peter 3:7). Unfortunately, traditional teaching about the roles in the home has painted a picture unlike that which has been given to us as *ezer kenegdo*—a strong helper who is a counterpart to man, visible in His sight. Cultural norms and teachings have distorted many men's view of how essential a woman's partnership truly is, which has been one of the major contributors to the lack of advancement of kingdom men on earth.

God-Blessed

God created humankind to rule. Yet a man, and likewise a woman, is to rule according to the design God has established. When he does, he can expect to be blessed. Because after God created man and commissioned him to rule, God concluded the process by giving a blessing.

"God blessed them and said to them, 'Be fruitful and multiply, and fill the earth, and subdue it; and rule over the fish of the sea and over the birds of the sky and over every living thing that moves on the earth' " (Genesis 1:28).

A blessing is a popular thing these days. Everybody wants to be blessed. But a blessing isn't simply more stuff or more money. I know plenty of people who have a bigger house and a bigger salary than they have ever had before, but now they are even more miserable than ever. A blessing isn't merely getting everything you think you might want. Rather, a blessing is the capacity to experience, enjoy, and extend the goodness of God in your life.

A blessing is never only about you. It is always intended to include you, but it is also intended to go through you to others. Too many Christians today want God to bless them without being willing for God to bless others through them. What they are doing is actually limiting the blessing in their own lives, because God always blesses as a way of extending that blessing to more than just the person being blessed. If you are not willing to be a blessing to others through what God has given you, then why should He consider you as a good candidate for a blessing?

When God blessed Adam and Eve in the garden, He told them to be fruitful and multiply. Then He enabled them to fill the earth and extend the blessing He had given them throughout the land and to those who came after them. Not only that, but another way that God also blessed them was that He provided resources in the place, the garden, where they were supposed to rule. When God called humankind to rule, He did not call him to rule something that God had not already made the provision for how it would be done. That is a true definition of a blessing. A blessing is when God supplies you for your calling. It is when God provides all that is needed for you to accomplish all that is under your rule.

You know that you have been blessed when you are able to enjoy the goodness of God despite the trials and tribulations associated with what you are doing. And you have access to enough strength, assets, and capacity to do what you have been called to do.

The powerful truth to remember about ruling your world, men, is that God always supplies for the world He wants you to rule. A lot of men are going out to try to rule a world, or a sphere of influence, that was never appointed by God for them to rule. Or they are not ruling according to God's divine blueprint. And they are wondering why they are tired and frustrated all the time. They are wondering why it is not working out. It is not working out because they are not in the right garden where God has placed them. They have wandered into someone else's garden, outside of their own.

Once you leave what He has called you to do, and you try to rule other people's worlds, you are on your own. God is not interested in helping you advance your own kingdom, someone else's kingdom, or to rule someone else's world. God has a kingdom, and in it He has designated specific authority for specific individuals to work according to a specific plan to best advance His kingdom.

9

ACCESSING YOUR AUTHORITY

In January 2010, I struggled with a battle that went on way too long. After several weeks, in fact after nearly the entire month, it looked like the enemy was gaining too much ground.

So I did what I hate to do.

I called my doctor.

It took only a few minutes for me to tell him how I had been feeling all month long—my head was plugged, my throat was scratchy, my body ached, I was feverish, I had chills, and my eyes watered. I explained to him that I had gone to the local drugstore and tried a number of so-called solutions.

It wasn't until the doctor addressed the reality that either what I thought to be my problem was not my problem, or my problem was worse than I imagined, that I was given what I really needed. After analyzing my situation, my doctor took out a piece of paper and scribbled something on it. I then drove myself to the store and handed the paper to the pharmacist. He quickly filled my prescription and said, "Tony"—by then I was on a first-name basis with everyone in there—"you are going to be okay."

While I had been in the store numerous times before, I had never been authorized to go to the spot where they provide medicine that is not available to the general public. Prior to receiving my doctor's written prescription, I had not been authorized to claim what I really needed. But once I had been authorized and followed the instructions on the prescription, I was back to full health and ready to take on anything and everything that life brought my way.

What is often true of our bodies is also true with our lives. Something is not right in our personal lives, homes, families, or jobs, but what we are using to try to address it does not seem to be working. The problem is not that we are insincere. It is not that we haven't been trying to fix what is broken. It is not that we haven't spent enough valuable time and resources on a solution. It is not even that we don't go to church, read our Bibles, or pray. It is just that we are using an over-the-counter method to address what only God has the authority to grant.

> *This principle . . . can make or break a man. This truth is why you should love being a man.*

Men, we are about to head into a discussion on a topic that, because it has been frequently misinterpreted and misused, we have often failed to take full advantage of the power of its truth. This principle, depending on how a man aligns himself with it, can make or break a man. This truth is why you should love being a man.

We are going to talk about the kingdom. And we are going to talk about authority. But most important, we are going to talk about what is referred to in theological circles as the *dominion covenant* (see Genesis 1:26–28; 9:1–5; Matthew 28:18–20) a part of which is what I like to simply call *naming*. The dominion covenant is the manifestation of God's kingdom principles operating within society. In this specific principle of *naming*, God has written down a prescription that places a significant amount of influence and authority squarely in the hands of men. If and when you use this prescription according to the instructions that come with it, you have the ability to impact your realm in more ways than you may have even imagined.

Naming.

This is what it is all about. This is what, depending on how you use it or don't use it, can bring you your greatest joy or your deepest sorrow. This is what separates the men from the boys. Because as a kingdom man, you get to name things. Better yet, as a man under God's authority, you get to name things and watch God bring them into being. That is real power. That is real dominion. That is capitalizing on every fiber and every sinew of who you were created to be.

Naming.

It is your right. It is your responsibility. And it is your destiny.

Naming

To fully grasp the significance of naming something, you first need to understand the context of names within biblical cultures. In Old Testament times, a name was more than simply nomenclature. It was, rather, a replica and revelation of the individual or thing itself.

A name is so important in biblical settings that there are frequent mentions throughout Scripture of God himself changing someone's name to reflect a new reality. Abram, which means *father*, was changed to Abraham meaning *father of a multitude of nations* (Genesis 17:5). Jacob, whose original name meant *grabber of the heel* and *deceitful* (Genesis 25:26), had his name changed to Israel after wrestling with God. His new name, Israel, means *one who prevails* (Genesis 32:28). In the book of Hosea, God changed the names of Hosea's son and daughter to signify the change in His relationship with them from Lo-ammi meaning *not My people* (Hosea 1:9) and Lo-Ruhamah meaning *she has not obtained compassion* (Hosea 1:6) to Ammi and Ruhammah, which mean *my people* and *one who is shown compassion* (Hosea 2:1).

In Scripture, a name often denoted and connoted purpose, authority, makeup, and ownership. A name was frequently seen as an actual equivalent of a person or thing. Jesus said that He had made God's "name known to them, and will make it known" (John 17:26). He was referencing more than just sounds put together in a word. Jesus, having come to earth in the flesh, unveiled God's heart, mind, will, character, and being through the revelation of His name.

Whether used as *shem* in Hebrew or as *onoma* in Greek, the translated word that shows up over one thousand times in Scripture[1] that we call *name* routinely carries with it power, responsibility, purpose, and authority. A name not only expresses the essence and significance of the being or thing, a name—when duly authorized—accesses the capacity intrinsic within it. To be in the position to name something—to give something or someone its identifying component—communicates ownership, responsibility, and the exercising of authority over it. A name predetermines and establishes the expectations for what that thing or person is to become.

A key element, however, in practicing and perfecting the art of naming, which we are about to look at in Genesis, is tied directly to the rightful alignment of a man under God. This is not a blank check to name, claim, and gain whatever it is that you want. Unless attached to the overarching governance of God according to His kingdom agenda, the use of naming may actually leave a man vulnerable to loss. This is because without that name being tied to the legitimacy of its root, its declaration carries no weight.

In Acts we read about a situation where Jewish men were attempting to cast out demons in the names of both Paul and Jesus. The demons refused to leave, however, since the men had not been given the authority to use Christ's name. The men had not placed themselves in a position under His rule; therefore, His name carried no ability to affect change. As a result, the Jewish men found themselves overpowered so that "they fled out of that house naked and wounded" (Acts 19:15–17).

As we will see in the following passage, Adam did not set out to name anything and everything that he came across. Adam wasn't the prototype for what many now mistakenly believe is their right to "name and claim" whatever they choose. Adam named that which God "brought" to him within the realm that God had already placed him in and had declared that he should rule. Adam named that which came under the dominion and within the domain God had given him. It was Adam's response to what God had brought to him. Authority in naming is a delicate dance between sovereignty and personal responsibility, like a quick-footed running back zipping in and out of potential tackles. But it is a dance—if done correctly—that will forever change your world. Let's look at Genesis 2:19: "Out of the ground the LORD God formed every beast of the field and every bird of the sky, and brought *them* to the man to see what he would call them; and whatever the man called a living creature, that was its name."

Did you catch that? Whatever Adam called it, *that was its name*. No discussion. No explanation. No alteration. What Adam named it, it became.

A name is never just a word. A name is a revelation and an expectation. In the garden, God had given Adam a calling to study, analyze, classify, and name whatever it was that God brought him. Through this process, Adam took ownership and exercised authority in determining what each thing would be called as part of the mandate he had been given to rule.

Calling First

One important thing to note in this situation—and something that is often over-shadowed by our focus on Adam, Eve, the serpent, and the fruit—is that before God ever made a woman, He gave Adam a calling. He gave Adam a job. God did not create Adam and Eve at the same time. He created Adam first as His lead subordinate. Eve did not come into play until after Adam had fulfilled his calling of naming that which God had brought him, as well as beginning the process of managing on God's behalf. In other words, the man was to know and practice responsibility under God before he was given responsibility over a woman. Adam measured his greatness by his calling, not by his marriage.

> *Before God ever made a woman, He gave Adam a calling.*

Yet when God eventually did bring Adam his wife, it was Adam's responsibility to name her as well.

> The Lord God fashioned into a woman the rib, which He had taken from the man, and brought her to the man. The man said, "This is now bone of my bones, and flesh of my flesh; she shall be called Woman, because she was taken out of Man." (Genesis 2:22–23)

Adam carefully chose the name *woman*, based not only on the biological reality of how Eve came into being, but also as a reflection of divine order and design. Her name was more than a classification; it encapsulated themes of function and purpose. One of the greatest illustrations of the comprehensive nature of naming is revealed through this name "Woman, because she was taken out of Man." Since Adam was created before Eve and given the role as head over a woman while under God, and because she was taken from man, manifested in the name he gave her.

As the man, Adam was positioned to either be a goat or a hero through the decisions that he and his wife made. With the authority to name comes influence and power—something most men gravitate toward—but authority also comes with responsibility. Many men focus on the influence and power while ignoring the responsibility. Yet a kingdom man who aligns himself under the lordship of Jesus Christ will be accountable for all that composes his role. God named Adam. Adam named Eve, demonstrating the flow of accountability and responsibility.

I'll never forget when my daughter Priscilla got married a number of years ago. Prior to her marriage, Priscilla was under my guidance, rule, and authority as her father. She was Priscilla Evans. She had my name. Yet when Priscilla decided to shift kingdoms—when she aligned herself under her husband as her new head, he gave her a new last name. Along with giving her his name, it now meant that Priscilla's husband was to be responsible for her provision, protection, and overall spiritual guidance.

The problem early on, though, was that two weeks after Priscilla had gotten married, she called me and said, "Dad, I need some money."

I said, "Priscilla, go ask your husband."

Priscilla quickly answered, "But, Dad, you're my father."

To which I just as quickly replied, "When I was your head, I was responsible. But now that you have shifted to a new realm and have been given a new name, your husband is responsible. Ask him. And if you still need money after asking him, have him ask me."

Naming not only comes with authority but also with responsibility.

As a pastor, I have had the opportunity to officiate hundreds of weddings. No two weddings are ever the same except for the radiance that glows on the face of the bride and the anticipation on the face of the groom. Now, I know what the groom is anticipating, and so do you. His mind has already fast-forwarded a few hours ahead. And maybe the bride is focused there as well, but most likely she is glowing because she believes that the man she is about to marry is going to provide her with safety, security, companionship, and care. In light of the hope and expectation of all of those things, she will gladly allow him to rename her. She will take his name because with his name comes the promise for a better future with him than she would have had without him.

In 2011 I had the privilege of delivering a message at the Dallas Cowboys quarterback Tony Romo's wedding. As you might imagine, the place was alive with beauty and energy. Every tiny detail had been attended to ahead of time with the most careful thought. When it came time for the new bride to say her vows and relinquish her name, no one heard her object to receiving the new name,

Romo. Rather, she took the new name with the honor and enthusiasm that so many others have when they run out to identify with that name by buying a jersey with *Romo* on the back. The name means something. And when a name means something good, it brings about good in the life of the one who receives it.

One of the tensions, though, that men often face, particularly with their wives, is that men often give their name without knowing what giving a name means. If a man is not sure who he is, if he has not fulfilled or begun to fulfill his calling before he enters a relationship, he can expect to bring confusion into that relationship. His wife will end up confused about her name simply because he, as a man, is confused about his.

This truth applies not only in homes, but also in careers. Some men have not made it further in their careers because they fail to know their own name and calling, and the men don't realize that they have the authority to name other things. They think that somehow they are satisfied with the little piece of the world they have found. Or they confuse what God is bringing to them with what they want Him to bring, so they name the wrong things and, as a result, do not see them come into being. God authorizes dominion only when a man functions as a subordinate to Him and the governance He gives. If a man is trying to do his own thing, or promote his own agenda in his own kingdom, he will lack the authority to name.

> *Some men have not made it further in their careers because they fail to know their own name and calling.*

Get It Straight

Men, I want you to get this truth. I want you to think differently because of it. I want you to begin to think in terms of your divinely given authority and responsibility. Take hold of creation; grab the piece of creation that God has for you to name. No feeling can compare to seeing God bring you things that you would have had to work your fingers to the bone to try to get. God brings them to you instead because they are yours to name, or you have already named them. Nothing is quite like seeing God open doors that have been slammed shut.

As I mentioned earlier, I started a church in my house. Eventually, we moved to holding it at an apartment, then later on God provided in a miraculous way for us to buy a small A-frame building on Camp Wisdom Road in Dallas, which is a story in and of itself. Yet it was around that time in my spiritual growth and development that this principle of naming became a part of how I functioned. I'll talk more about it in the next chapter, but I literally started naming property and land all alongside this small A-frame building. I would look at a piece of land, and I would name it for God's kingdom because God had said, "Let them rule." And since I intended to use it in connection with something that God could benefit from and that He would get the glory out of, I exercised a kingdom-approach to naming. As a result, God added land to our church property.

> "God, I name that. I name this entire place for the good of others and for Your glory."

One particular piece of land that I drove by for years was an old abandoned mansion sitting on twenty pristine acres in the heart of urban Dallas. It was in an exquisite location. In fact, the film for which Robert Duvall won his only Oscar as Best Actor, *Tender Mercies*,[2] was filmed there. The film centered on the themes of restoration, spiritual hope, family, and healing—a foreshadowing of things to come.

I remember driving by this property one day and deciding to pull my car right up in front of the vacant and now run-down building. Years had passed since God had put it on my heart that this building was going to be used for His glory. So while looking at the building, I said, "God, I name that. I name this entire place for the good of others and for your glory. We don't have the money for it right now, but God, hold it for us. Because I name it in Jesus' name."

Not too long after that day, sitting in my car and staring at that building, God revealed a way for us to get it. And now that land and that building, once used as a film set, have become a pregnancy center where the message of restoration and new beginnings is given to teen girls in crisis every single day.

Men, I want you to own this principle because I have seen it pay huge dividends in my own life beyond what I can even express in the pages of this book. I have seen it so much that I now go throughout my day looking for something that

I can name, and then I watch in anticipation for God to bring it to fruition. Each day comes with a spirit of expectation because I have seen Him do so much already in response to the practice of this truth. It's important, though, to realize that naming does not mean claiming anything and everything that you want. Neither is it naming something solely for your personal benefit. Naming—like everything a man is supposed to do—is always tied to God's glory and the expansion of His kingdom. It is assigning divine involvement based on how God's revealed will and Word says He will be involved.

Does this require an intimate and abiding relationship with God so you are attuned to what He is bringing to you—either in your thoughts, across your path, in your prayers, or in the Word—to name? Absolutely. Is it worth every effort put into spiritual growth and a personal relationship in knowing and experiencing Him? Without question. The process of naming things is confirmed objectively by God's Word and subjectively by the inner witness of the Holy Spirit and confirmation of circumstances. So the closer you are to God and His Word, the closer you are to knowing and naming what God has destined for you.

When you get the opportunity to name things and watch God bring them into being, that means that even God is respecting your manhood. God is free to respect your manhood when you respect His Godhood. That's how it works. That is how you experience kingdom success. Living as a kingdom man is in large part a state of mind. It is an understanding that you are not of this world. You represent another kingdom and serve the one true King. In any kingdom, what the King says will happen *does* happen. That is authority. As a kingdom man, it is your mission to know God fully and seek to advance His glory. When you do, He will lead you and direct you according to what He wants to give you. He will bring you things to name. And, then, when you name them, He will bring them into being.

The problem facing many men today in connection with the dominion mandate is their understanding of what kingdom success really is. A misunderstanding of success will lead a man to name things illegitimately or keep a man from advancing in the realm and direction that God has for him. People define success in multiple ways. Some people define it as prominence or holding a high position. Others define it as financial gain. Still others define it as relationships and the achievements within their families. Yet I know, and you probably do too, a number of miserable people in high positions with what the world considers func-tioning families and large bank accounts. In addition, prominence may last only a minute in this day and age. Things change.

Kingdom success runs much deeper than the width of a wallet, the square footage of a home, or the smiles in a photograph hanging on a wall. Success has to do with fulfilling the reason why you were both born and born again. It involves living out your ordained reason for being for God's glory, your good, and the benefit of others.

Success means fulfilling your destiny.

10

TOUCHING HEAVEN, CHANGING EARTH

It doesn't matter how much money you have when you die, how many people know your name, or what position you held. If you never got around to doing and being what your destiny is, then all you were was a successful failure. Success means arriving at God's prescribed destination for you while having the capacity to experience, enjoy, and extend His goodness in your life.

Friend, you have a destination. You have a destiny that God has ordained for you and offers to you. You are not just here to take up space, water the lawn, and watch television. You are here for more. You are here to rule—and to rule well.

The problem, though, is that although Adam, and men through him, was endowed with the mandate and authority to rule his realm and name what God brought him by his position of headship, Adam fumbled the ball. When the leader became the responder and ate the fruit given to him by Eve, he dropped the ball. In fact, Satan didn't even have to strip it out of his hands. Adam simply dropped it, then he ran to the stands attempting to hide from God.

Adam's fumble would not only affect his relationship, but also his location. It would not only affect his career, but also his children to come. Adam's cataclysmic fumble carried with it personal, financial, familial, and societal repercussions that have played out ever since in the lives of all men who have come after him.

This is because at the moment of Adam's fumble, the kingdom of darkness ruled by Satan issued a challenge to the kingdom of light ruled by God. At that moment our world became the battleground for an epic war as Satan laid claim to God's creation, humankind. With this newly gained momentum, Satan went on the offense attempting to dethrone the Creator of all. Yet what Adam lost in the garden, Christ regained at the cross. And unless you understand the theology of spiritual authority, you will continue to play life on defense, reacting to another ruler, rather than running over him as you rule.

Paul, in Colossians, summarized the elements of spiritual authority most clearly when he wrote:

> See to it that no one takes you captive through philosophy and empty deception, according to the tradition of men, according to the elementary principles of the world, rather than according to Christ. For in Him all the fullness of Deity dwells in bodily form, and in Him you have been made complete, and He is the head over all rule and authority," (Colossians 2:8–10)

Not only is Jesus Christ the head over all rule and authority, but He has also "disarmed the rulers and authorities. . . having triumphed over them through Him" (Colossians 2:15). When Christ disarmed Satan, he removed the authority Satan had gained in the garden over humankind. Satan still has power, but he has no authority. There is a big difference between those two. Just like there is a big difference between someone standing in front of you holding a loaded gun and someone standing in front of you holding a gun that is not loaded. The person with the loaded gun ought to evoke a completely contrary response than the person with the empty gun.

The problem, though, that arises in a situation like that is how to tell if the gun is loaded or not. Satan still wields a gun, and without a believer's comprehension of spiritual authority, Satan's empty gun continues to pressure and intimidate. Yet, the truth is, his gun is empty. With Christ's death on the cross, God removed the bullets and "rescued us from the domain of darkness and transferred us to the kingdom of His beloved Son" (Colossians 1:13).

Stand Against the Enemy

I hear what you are saying, though. You are asking, "Tony, if Satan has been defeated, then why am I always playing defense? Why are there issues in my life that I can't seem to overcome and things I can't seem to name? If Satan has already lost, why does he seem so powerful?" Satan *is* defeated. But, like a person beaten in life, he doesn't want to go down alone. He is still fighting, and what you believe about his authority makes an enormous difference in how you respond to it.

As I write this chapter, the Dallas Mavericks have just won the NBA Finals (in 2011). It was an exciting game to watch. Yet over all of the years I have worked with the Mavericks, they haven't always come in that close at the end. In fact, some seasons they missed making the play-offs by a country mile. They were defeated long before the season even concluded. Yet during their final game, they would still play with a passion for victory. Why? Because dealing a late-season loss to a rival team might affect that team's chances of becoming champions. In other words, "We may not be going to the play-offs, but we're going to do everything we can to make sure that you don't either."

> *Satan's goal is to rob us of our spiritual "championship bid" and drag us down to his level.*

Likewise, Satan's goal is to rob us of our spiritual "championship bid" and drag us down to his level. If you are saved, he can't drag you into hell, but he can sure make you experience hell on earth. Satan knows what Paul knew—that God has "blessed us with every spiritual blessing in the heavenly *places* in Christ" (Ephesians 1:3). Satan understands our potential; he knows what God can make of us. He even knows the authority that each of us has in connection to Jesus Christ. And Satan is committed to seeing to it that we never reach our destiny.

Satan has power. He has the power to deceive, the power to intimidate, the power to persuade, and even the power to destroy, but his power is limited because he doesn't have authority. Jesus has the authority. Shortly before Christ ascended into heaven after having been raised from the dead, He declared, "All authority has been given to Me in heaven and on earth" (Matthew 28:18). Jesus has complete authority.

There are two major Greek words meaning authority used in the Bible: *dynamis*[1] and *exousia*.[2] The first word, *dynamis*, is best translated into English as a generic term for power. *Dynamis* power is like a loaded gun. In the hand of a policeman, it represents legitimate power, but in the hand of a criminal, it is illegitimate. The gun remains the same, but the use of its power changes.

It is not *dynamis* that Jesus speaks of in Matthew 28:18, it is *exousia*. *Exousia* means power, but it means power in rightful hands. *Exousia* is the power of our elected officials to govern us or the power of a policeman to arrest a criminal. For example, the players on a football field are bigger, tougher, stronger, and can overpower any of the referees calling the game, but since the players have only *dynamis*, they are overpowered by the referees' *exousia*. *Exousia* is legal power. When Jesus said that all authority—all *exousia*—had been given to Him, He was saying He had legal, rightful power. Essentially, He was saying that He had the authority with the power.

Men, you are a subject in God's kingdom, so Satan no longer has legal authority over you. You don't need to live playing defense or being afraid. Jesus has declared that all authority has been given to Him, and in Him, as a believer, you *have been made complete*. You are *seated with Him* where He rules *in the heavenly places*. The only way Satan can strip you of your authority to name that which God has placed in your dominion and watch it come into being is to get you out from under Christ's authority. Satan wants to get you out of alignment and the covering that comes with aligning yourself under the headship of Jesus Christ. As long as you are in alignment, men, you have access to all the *exousia* you need to do all that God has destined you to do.

Yet we all know that it is possible to have legal rights that you do not use. It is possible to have something legislated that is never enforced. It is possible to be free but still act like a slave. It is even possible to be delivered but still act like a prisoner of spiritual war simply because you have not put action to what has been legalized. The cross of Jesus Christ has legalized your authority to carry out your dominion, but for that which is legalized to be put into action, it must first be realized.

Praying with Power

One often-neglected way of realizing what God has authorized is through prayer. Now don't flip to the next chapter just because I brought up prayer. In my opinion, prayer is the most under-used tool in the arsenal of a kingdom man. But because we think it must be done a certain way, at a certain time, for a certain length of time, and about certain things, we often don't do it at all.

Not only is the key to prayer in having faith like a child, but it is also in knowing what you ought to pray. If you pray what you ought to pray, you will get what you pray for. Jesus says, "Whatever you ask in My name, that will I do, so that the Father may be glorified in the Son. If you ask Me anything in My name, I will do *it*" (John 14:13–14). To ask for something in Jesus' name means to ask according to what Jesus would sanction, or what He would do. It is best explained by Christ's words, "If you abide in Me, and My words abide in you, ask whatever you wish, and it will be done for you" (John 15:7).

Prayer is the most under-used tool in the arsenal of a kingdom man.

As long as you are asking according to the will of God, you will get everything that you ask for. The secret in praying is not necessarily in how long you pray or what kind of fancy words that you pray it is in discovering God's will for your life and then asking for it. When you find out what God wants, what His heart is about, then your prayers will line up with Him. If His words are abiding in you, His wishes will become your wishes and He will "give you the desires of your heart" (Psalm 37:4) because your desires will be His desires.

Prayer isn't about sending up some words to God. It involves knowing God, listening to Him, and aligning your heart with His. When a kingdom man is properly aligned, his prayers will get answered. And when you start to see your prayers getting answered, praying doesn't remain the burden or ethereal duty that so many of us make it out to be. Rather, it becomes a conversation—transactional in nature in many regards. Men rarely leverage the power of prayer, and, as a result, most men are not living out the fullness of their destiny.

Going through college and seminary when you are married with children can take its toll on anyone's finances. Ours were no different. For years, my wife, Lois, performed miracles with our money to make it stretch enough to put food on the table and clothes on our children. But I remember one morning in particular when Lois and I were sharing breakfast together and she looked very discouraged. "Tony, I just can't do this anymore. It's too hard," she said.

We spent some time talking about the strain that living on such a limited budget with four kids in the home was putting on her. I could see that, even though she wanted to support me and believed in God's call on my life, she had reached a point where the burden was too heavy.

I was also convinced of my call, and even though I was a much younger Christian at the time, I also believed that God said He would provide for that which He asked me to do. To see my wife at a point where she was telling me she couldn't go on like this was confusing because it made me wonder how God could let it get to this point. He had said He would supply.

So I decided at that point, knowing that my primary responsibility under God as a man was to meet the emotional, physical, and spiritual needs of my family first, that I would drop out of seminary to get a full-time job. I told Lois of my plan and asked her one thing, "What would it take for you to receive today in order for you to support me continuing in seminary and not dropping out?"

> *Unless we got $500 that very day, I had told Lois I would drop out of seminary.*

I asked for a number, a specific amount.

Lois thought about it a while and then said, "$500."

Now, keep in mind, this was in the 1970s when $500 was an awful lot of money. And unless we got $500 that very day, I had told Lois I would drop out of seminary.

So guess what I did. You better believe it. I prayed.

God had called me to prepare for the ministry and had led me to this seminary, and I was convinced that I should stay. But He had also called me to be a husband who took care of his wife, and Lois said she needed $500 that day for her to feel equipped and enabled to support me to stay.

Prayer was all I had at that point. So pray is what I did.

Making my way to the seminary for what looked like might be my last day of classes, I decided not to tell anyone about my early morning conversation with Lois. I had told God. I had prayed. That was going to have to be enough.

After attending my classes, I went to the mailroom to get my mail. And when I opened my box, I saw something that looked like money. There inside my box were five $100 bills attached to a note from a man named John who said that God had told him to give this to me today. It was exactly the amount Lois had told me she needed, and the amount that I had asked God to provide.

Power Play

You don't need to be a super-spiritual, sinless saint to maximize prayer. But you do need to know God intimately and rightly align yourself under Him. When James wrote about the power of prayer, he referred to Elijah who "was a man with a nature like ours" (James 5:17). Elijah wasn't a superhero. He was a man. He was not perfect. No one is perfect. But Elijah "prayed earnestly that it would not rain, and it did not rain on the earth for three years and six months. Then he prayed again, and the sky poured rain and the earth produced its fruit" (James 5:17–18).

Elijah was an ordinary man with a nature like yours and mine. Because He was a righteous man rightly aligned under God, this ordinary man got heaven to move on earth. As we read about in 1 Kings, there was a problem on Earth so Elijah called on heaven, and heaven responded. Heaven responded because Elijah was praying in line with God's Word. "Now it happened *after* many days that the Word of the LORD came to Elijah in the third year, saying, 'Go, show yourself to Ahab, and I will send rain on the face of the earth'" (1 Kings 18:1).

The land in and around Samaria had been experiencing a three-year drought. Vegetation and animals depend on rain from above, so a three-year drought can devastate a nation. The drought had resulted because of the disobedience of the people and their turn toward Baal rather than to God. But after three years, God told Elijah that He would make it rain again.

So when Elijah prayed, he prayed according to what God had already said. He prayed according to what he had already been told would happen:

> Elijah said to Ahab, "Go up, eat and drink; for there is the sound of the
> roar of a *heavy* shower." So Ahab went up to eat and drink. But Elijah went
> up to the top of Carmel; and he crouched down on the earth and
> put his face between his knees. (1 Kings 18:41–42)

Elijah got into a position of prayer and remained there while he instructed his servant to go look toward the sea to see if the rain clouds were coming. The servant went and returned seven times while Elijah stayed crouched on Mt. Carmel. God had declared to Elijah already that it was going to rain, but no rain hit the earth until Elijah called it down from heaven. Prayer ushered down what God had already intended to do. It didn't make God do something He hadn't planned on doing, but it brought it about. That is the power of prayer. Its secret is in knowing what God intends to do.

An interesting thing about Elijah's prayer on the mountain was how he did it. It says that he "crouched down . . . and put his face between his knees." While that image may not mean much to us today, it probably meant a lot in the Old Testament times because it was a common position a pregnant woman would get in when she was ready to give birth. They didn't have the sophisticated rooms and stir-ups like hospitals do today. Most women would need to crouch down, bend over, and push through the agonizing pain. They would travail, pushing out what had grown within.

> *That is the power of prayer. Its secret is in knowing what God intends to do.*

When Elijah got down in a crouching position, he was in a travailing position because he was attempting to pull down out of heaven what was ready to be born—rain. Six times the servant returned from the sea to tell Elijah that there was no rain on the horizon. Each time Elijah remained as he was, travailing to receive that which God had promised. Eventually, on the seventh trip to the sea, the servant returned and said, "'Behold, a cloud as small as a man's hand is coming up from the sea'" (1 Kings 18:44). The cloud was crowning, and the rain was about to pour forth out of the skies.

What Elijah did through prayer was reach in and grab what God had already told him He would give.

Elijah's example means to us, as kingdom men, that a kingdom man is to labor in God's presence until he gets a specific answer to a specific request designed to manifest God's will in history. He doesn't quit just because nothing is happening at the moment. Like Jacob who wrestled with God all night until he got a response from heaven, men are to wrestle with God until heaven responds.

What God says He wants to do doesn't always happen on Earth just because He declared it to be. Often, God is waiting on our labor to bring it down. This is because He has given dominion to man. Prayer is the human means of entering the supernatural realm to have heaven visit Earth. The invisible gets pulled down through prayer.

Since God responds to the fervent prayer of a righteous man, men must first make sure that they are spiritually in cadence with the Lord. Their prayers must be focused, specific, and intense—not casual or run-of-the-mill repetitions. The intensity and power of their prayer are also increased when they pray with their wives (Matthew 18:20).

What Victory Requires

Men, you have authority.

Use it.

Stop playing your relationship with God so safe.

A kingdom man must learn how to access God's authority to reach into heaven and bring heaven's authority to Earth.

It was a great honor that I received not too long ago to be asked by the Pittsburgh Steelers home office to speak to the team at the chapel service the night before their eighth trip to the Super Bowl. Only the Dallas Cowboys had been to the big game as many times. And although that was a great game to watch, I imagine that few of us can forget watching the Steelers in Super Bowl XLIII, when they claimed the NFL record for the most Super Bowl wins at six, which they did in 2009.[3]

Not only did the game set that record, but also the 100-yard interception return for a touchdown by Steelers' linebacker James Harrison is still the longest play ever in Super Bowl history.[4] Coasting into the fourth quarter with a 20–7 lead, though, most of us probably thought that the Steelers would pull this one off without much drama. The game had been fairly uneventful up until then. But that was before Cardinals quarterback Kurt Warner put 16 unanswered points on the board in the last 15 minutes of the season.

Only one drive remained for the Steelers to offer their response.

Which they did.

And what a response it was.

With 2:37 seconds on the clock and two of their three allotted timeouts still in their pocket, Ben Roethlisberger, completed three passes and a 4-yard run to move the Steelers into enemy ground. Yet with the clock ticking and the scoreboard looming, the Steelers stayed calm. There was plenty of time to get things done. Roethlisberger had been successful in his previous two passes to Santonio Holmes to get them where they needed to go, so he threw a strike to Holmes again—this time completing, because of Holmes' run, a 40-yard conversion.

Less than a minute remained on the clock while the six yards between the Steelers and the end zone taunted them to settle for a field goal, and a subsequent tie. But the Steelers wanted more.

First down and goal to go, Roethlisberger threw to Holmes in the back of the end zone. He threw it high. Holmes couldn't come up with the ball. Ending up on the ground instead, his head down, fists beating together, Holmes knew that it was now or never.

> *Holmes stretched, grabbed the victory, and brought it down for the game-icing touchdown.*

Second and goal to go, Roethlisberger looked for Holmes again—same location, other side. With three defenders around him and the possibility of a tie still within their grasp, Roethlisberger threw the ball high yet again aiming at only a sliver of room in the end zone. No reason to risk an interception. However, in doing so, he also made a touchdown a nearly impossible feat to come by.

Regardless, what happened next is now known as one of the greatest catches in Super Bowl history. In an uncanny ability, Holmes somehow managed to reach his hands high enough to catch, and control, the ball while also keeping not just one, but both, feet inbounds and on the ground. Standing on nothing but his toes, Holmes stretched, grabbed the victory, and brought it down for the game-icing touchdown.

With that, Pittsburgh took the lead. And a few plays and not too many seconds on the clock later, Roethlisberger took a knee. The Super Bowl war of 2009 had been decided.

Men, you are in a war. You are in a spiritual conflict. You are in a battle of epic proportions. Others have lined up to face you, and their only goal is to keep you from advancing God's kingdom down the field of life. Because of them, the passes thrown to you can't always be within your grasp. In fact, often because of the nature of the battle, they are thrown high. Yet you have been given all that you need to reach up into heaven and bring victory down to earth.

God never said it would be easy. He never said there wouldn't be missed passes along the way. But what He did say is that the victory is yours if you will reach up and grab it. And later finish this war on a knee.

Prayer. It is a kingdom man's primary weapon of warfare.

With it, you will touch heaven and change earth.

11

KEYS TO CLAIMING YOUR TERRITORY

The 2008 economic crunch that crippled our nation in so many ways ushered in a number of vicissitudes in life. Many employers were forced to reduce the number of jobs on their payroll. Manufacturers searched for more efficient methods of producing their goods. Charitable giving dropped, even causing churches to feel the impact, as a large number of them put a freeze on new hires and cut back on expenses.

One of the most impactful actions that my church took was the installation of a motion detector lighting system. With multiple facilities in our complex, keeping the lights on at all times during the day and even some at night was an enormous expense and a drain on kingdom resources. But with the installation of the new system, we reduced our electrical costs by a staggering amount.

As I'm sure you are aware, the motion detector system essentially turns off the lights after a certain amount of time passes without sensing any movement. If and when someone walked into the vicinity of the motion detector, the lights would then come back on.

In many ways, the motion detector lighting system is similar to a kingdom man practicing his right to rule. Like the electrical company that has entirely supplied the electricity needed to fully power every light in our buildings, God has fully supplied all that you need to exercise the authority He has given to you. Yet God is not going to force that authority and power on you. When God delegated the management of earth to humankind, He placed men as a steward over His creation. With that provision, God empowered man with the right to make decisions. While these decisions could be made independent of or dependent on God, He gave a certain sphere of freedom in which to make them. God did not turn over total autonomy, but He did supply relative autonomy.

The idea of relative autonomy is simply that the degree to which humankind ruled under the authority of God is the same degree that he would receive the blessings and the power of God. This is similar to a man who walks within the vicinity of the motion detector lighting system receiving the light. Likewise the degree to which humankind ruled independently of God is the degree that the power would be withheld. Humankind would still be allowed to rule, but he would rule within a world of darkness and thus be faced with the repercussions of living without spiritual power.

> *God is waiting until He sees movement. He hits a moving target.*

So many men are waiting on God to move in regard to their personal problems, issues, or challenges, or in regard to their families, careers, or vision, yet God has already supplied all that is needed for them to rule. He is waiting on them to walk only in His ways so that He can turn on His power. God is waiting until He sees movement. He hits a moving target. Enacting the influence of dominion requires that you do something with the authority Christ has given to you.

Leave the Past Behind

Powerful principles for being a man of movement are found in Joshua 1. The Israelites had reached the point where they were about to advance into their destiny. They were about to cross over the Jordan and enter the Promised Land. Before they did so, though, God gave them instructions on how they were to face the enemies ahead and to exercise dominion over what He had given them. The first principle that we find to propel us into a life of movement is located in the first few verses:

Now it came about after the death of Moses the servant of the LORD, that the LORD spoke to Joshua the son of Nun, Moses' servant, saying,

"Moses My servant is dead; now therefore arise, cross this Jordan, you
and all this people, to the land which I am giving to them, to the sons
of Israel." (Joshua 1:1–2)

Rule number one, men: Leave the past behind. God told Joshua, "Moses my
servant is dead; now therefore arise . . ." In other words, Joshua, get up.

Moses was dead. Moses was gone. Joshua needed to be reminded that
although Moses had been a great man, a great leader, and had been instrumen-
tal in leading the Israelites into freedom, Moses had not gotten them into the
Promised Land. While Moses had been real, Moses was yesterday. It was time for
Joshua to get up and move on.

Some of you may not have gotten to your destination by now because you are
still too tied to Moses. Yet to move forward and attain your tomorrow, it is important that you say good-bye to yesterday. If God is going to take you where He
wants you to go, you can't be tethered to where you have been. A crucial principle
for advancing God's kingdom as a kingdom man is that if you are going to move
ahead, you are going to have to let go of the past.

All of us have pasts that involve the good, the bad, and the ugly. We can look
back over our shoulder and see the good things that have happened, the bad
things that we have done, and the ugly things that others have done to us. But that
was yesterday. That was the past. You have to let it go. You can learn from yesterday; just don't live in it. Because if you live in yesterday, then you are going to kill
tomorrow.

Whenever I go back to Baltimore to visit my parents, I inevitably run into
some of the guys whom I knew growing up. These men are still on the same corner talking the same noise that we used to talk as teenagers. The topic that dominates every discussion continues to be yesterday. I'm not saying that yesterday is
always a bad conversation topic, but you just don't want to get stuck there. You
don't want to live your life in the rearview mirror. A rearview mirror is important
when you are backing out or putting your car in reverse. It is even critical to peek
at every now and then as you move forward, but a much bigger piece of glass
called the windshield is more important than your rearview mirror. Where you
are going ought to be bigger than where you have been.

Many of us need to have a yesterday funeral. Even for the good things. Just because you made an A on yesterday's paper is no guarantee that you are going to pass today's test. Yesterday's victories will not carry you through today. Neither should yesterday's defeats dominate tomorrow.

> *If you are tied to a rope called yesterday, you can go only so far.*

Many of us need to have a funeral over yesterday because we are giving yesterday a power that it does not deserve. If you are tied to a rope called yesterday, you can go only so far. In spite of how painful and difficult it is, you must make a conscious decision to bury it. Let it go. Yes, it is fine to go visit it on Memorial Day and take it some flowers. But after that, move on.

God began His talk with Joshua by giving him an important reminder: Moses was gone. Then He told him to get up and get going. Remember, if Satan can keep you looking back, then he can keep you from moving forward.

Seize Your Spiritual Inheritance

The next rule for ruling your world taken from Joshua 1:2–4 is to seize your spiritual inheritance.

> Now therefore arise, cross this Jordan, you and all this people, to the land which I am giving to them, to the sons of Israel. Every place on which the sole of your foot treads, I have given it to you, just as I spoke to Moses. From the wilderness and this Lebanon, even as far as the great river, the river Euphrates, all the land of the Hittites, and as far as the Great Sea toward the setting of the sun will be your territory.

In this passage, God told Joshua that He had already marked out where Joshua was supposed to go. God had already staked out Joshua's inheritance. He told Joshua that from the wilderness to *as far as the Great Sea toward the setting of the sun* was for him and the Israelites. That was their land. That was their domain. God was giving it to them.

What was true for Joshua and the Israelites back then is also true for you today. God has already given you everything that you are destined to have. God has already determined everywhere that you are destined to go. Ephesians 1:3 tells us, "Blessed *be* the God and Father of our Lord Jesus Christ, who has blessed us with every spiritual blessing in the heavenly *places* in Christ."

Everything that God has destined for you, He has already given to you. It is located in the heavenly places, so now your job is to draw it down. What God says in the invisible spiritual realm gets pulled down through faith. Faith is never simply a feeling. Faith always involves your feet. It involves movement. God told Joshua that He had already given the land and the people in the land even before Joshua had stepped foot into it. Yet in living with kingdom authority meant Joshua had to actually go get it. Joshua had to do something. He had to move.

God has an inheritance and destiny for you as well. But one reason why you may not have experienced it yet is because your feet have not marched in tune with faith. God said to Joshua, "Every place on which the sole of your foot treads, I have given it to you . . ." When God gave the dominion mandate to humankind saying, "Let them rule," He gave access to His heavenly rule being executed by man on earth. Yet we all know that just because something is legalized does not mean that it has come into reality. What has been made available in eternity must be brought down into time. Men, God can give you something, yet you still do not have it simply because you did not walk on it—you did not go get it.

The Hebrew word used for tread, *darak,* refers to "a press."[1] It is the same word used to describe treading on grapes in a winepress. Long before sophisticated machinery was created to ease the process of turning grapes into wine, individuals would collect grapes from the vineyard and then tread, or walk, on top of them. They literally walked on the grapes to get the juice to come out of the grapes so the juice could then be fermented and turned into wine. By treading on the grapes, what had been locked inside of a grape was squeezed out.

When a kingdom man treads upon that which God has destined for him, He is not trying to get God to give him something. He is simply walking on that which God has already provided. There is a primitive view of faith in God that implies that a man sits down and does nothing, waiting on God to do everything. But actual faith is just the opposite. Faith means that you believe God so much that you are going to act on what He says. Faith is when you act as if God is telling the truth. Since Joshua believed God had given him the land, he walked in and claimed it.

One of the reasons that more men are not seeing the reality of what God has in store for them is either because they do not know that He has something in store for them, or they are not going out and grabbing it. God *is* the way-maker. He *is* our provider. He *does* miracles. But most of the time, God works through the very ordinary act of obeying whatever He has said to do.

Going to Get It

Not too long ago a member of our church sent me a care package for Clergy Appreciation Month. This member called to let me know that I should be expecting a package. A few days later, I got a note on my door from the mailman saying that the local post office had my package. It was my gift. My name was on it. But unless I took the steps to go get it, I would never have received it.

On a larger scale, I am reminded of the time when I began our church over thirty-five years ago. As I mentioned earlier, the church had gone from meeting in my home to meeting in an apartment facility, to eventually meeting at a public school. After a number of months in the public school, the school administrators informed us that our time there was about to run out. With only one hundred members at that point, we didn't have much of a budget with which to find a new location. Yet a little A-frame chapel came available for sale on Camp Wisdom Road in Dallas, and after much prayer and searching, I got a deep sense in my spirit that God had said He was giving us that building.

But the church selling the property wanted $200,000 for it. That might as well have been $2,000,000 to us since we had nothing. When I drove there one day to stand before it and ask God to give us the chapel, my eyes kept drifting beyond the small A-frame building. What continued to catch my attention was the more than one hundred acres of nearly all grass and trees surrounding it. Keep in mind that we didn't even have enough money for the chapel. Yet at that point, I believed God was making it clear to me that He planned to give us more than just the chapel—He was giving us all of the land surrounding it. I can't explain it. It was just one of those moments when "you know that you know" it is from God. One way He confirmed this to me was through time I had previously spent in His Word; He kept bringing to my mind the words found in Joshua 1, "Every place on which the sole of your foot treads, I have given it to you . . ."

So I started treading.

I literally walked from the A-frame building all the way up to the next intersection, nearly half of a mile. Then I crossed to the other side of the street and walked back down. All the while, I prayed, "Lord, please don't just give us that little chapel for a church to be used for your kingdom and your glory, God—but give us everything on both sides of the street." I was just a young pastor leading an urban church of one hundred people in the days before the term *megachurch* had even been invented. Yet so strong was my belief that God had given us that land that I walked every inch of the streets bordering it. I claimed it before I got it because I believed that God had given it. After thirty-five years, we now own all of the land that I walked on, including that little A-frame chapel. God has given us this land not only for a church, but also for one of the largest church-based com-

> *Paul specifically instructed us to "walk by faith" . . . because faith always involves our feet.*

munity outreach programs in the country, which now serves as a model for training other churches through our National Church Adopt-A-School Initiative ministry.

There is a reason that Paul specifically instructed us to "walk by faith" in 2 Corinthians 5:7 rather than to talk by faith. This is because faith always involves our feet. God had told Joshua that He had given him the whole land, but Joshua would be able to experience only the pieces of land that he walked on. If he wanted all of it, he needed to walk on all of it. God will let you have only what you claim. You must claim that which God has already provided.

The Christian life is not a video game to be played in virtual reality. It is a battle of flesh and blood. We are combatants in a real, tangible war. Paul told us, "Fight the good fight of faith; take hold of the eternal life to which you were called . . ." (1 Timothy 6:12). The Greek word, *epilambanomai*, translated into *take hold* literally means to seize.[2] Paul was writing to Timothy, a believer, and telling him that he is to *seize* all that is contained within his salvation. Far too often, it seems that men view the Christian life as a passive life they must live rather than as a gateway to the opportunity to conquer life's challenges. God has already given you, as a follower of Jesus Christ, all that He has stored up for you as His redeemed child, but you must seize it. You must go get it. Grab it, and do not let it go. There is an enemy whose goal in this war is to keep you from all that God has provided for you. To get it, you will need to push past him.

Start Moving Your Feet

What burdens my heart as a minister of God's Word is knowing that many men are going to reach heaven one day and see a stadium full of that which God had destined for them, but they never walked into to claim. So many people are living defeated lives when the victory has already been secured. So many men are living purposelessly when their destiny is rich with meaning and power. The Promised Land was God's legal inheritance given to Israel, but they still had to go in and possess it. They had to take responsibility to go get it. Responsibility is always tied to a blessing.

If you want to rule your world, you have to go get the world you have been destined to rule. Now, keep in mind, that you have to get it God's way, which always involves abiding in an intimate relationship with God through His Word so that the Holy Spirit gives and confirms God's leading and direction in your life. But even when you are certain of His leading, you still have to go get it. I wish I could shout right now from the top of the highest mountaintop, "Get up, men. Stop whining. Stop blaming. Stop fearing. Get up, and get what God has for you." We need you to. The kingdom of God needs each man to get up so we can advance God's kingdom together.

Each man has a territory that God has placed him in. Your territory is not the same as mine. Mine is not the same as yours. Ours is not the same as the man next door. But each of us has a territory. And whatever territory God has called you to exercise authority over and rule according to His kingdom principles and purpose, He has already provided all that you need to do so.

So many men fail to advance the vision God has put in their hearts because they are too busy trying to figure out how it is going to happen or how they will get what they need to carry it out. Yet God always provides for that which He purposes. That is why your priority should be to discover exactly what God's purpose is for you. When you get that, He will not only tell you how you are to achieve it, but He will also have already made the provisions for you to be and do what He has declared. Discovering your destiny is an integral part in turning it into reality.

God took Joshua and the Israelites into a land *flowing with milk and honey*. A land that flowed with both milk and honey simply means that it was already a highly productive land. Essentially, God used the sinners to dig the wells, shepherd the cattle, and make the land profitable before handing it over to the saints. Likewise, God is already working out how He is going to provide for you when you arrive at your destination. There is no need to worry about how you are going to accomplish the vision God has given you or how you are going to provide for the purpose He has put in your heart. When God has told you His plan for you, all you need to do is focus on taking whatever steps He is asking you to take now. And sometimes that is as simple as stepping out and walking. God's activity in your life is tied to your footsteps.

Focus on God, Not People

God knew that once Joshua put the past behind him, got up, and started going into the Promised Land that he was going to face a large number of enemies whose goal would be to stop him from reaching his destination. That is why God said:

No man will *be able to* stand before you all the days of your life. Just as I have been with Moses, I will be with you; I will not fail you or forsake you. Be strong and courageous, for you shall give this people possession of the land which I swore to their fathers to give them. Only be strong and very courageous. (Joshua 1:5–7)

In other words, God told Joshua that first he was to get up, and then he was to *man up*. The reason Joshua needed to man up was because people in the land were not going to like the fact that he just showed up. The Hittites, Jebusites, and Canaanites were going to resist Joshua's arrival. Knowing he would face tough opposition, God told Joshua ahead of time that none of it would be successful at preventing Joshua from receiving what God had told Joshua was his.

Unfortunately, many of us have been stopped from pursuing the fullness of God's purpose in our lives because of people. They might have been bad people, mean people, or even evil people, yet whatever they were, they were definitely larger and more powerful people. Maybe they had more money or more influence than you. Maybe you shrunk back from moving forward because they made your life miserable or intimidated you by their size, strength, or status. It might have been that they looked undefeatable since they had been functioning in a certain position for longer than you.

Yet what I want you to keep in mind as you face the giants in your own life is that people, on their best day, are still just people. And God is still God. Yet we often treat God like people and people like God, so we wind up not seeing God being God. We also wind up thinking that people are more than people. One of the greatest experiences that you can have is watching God override people, especially people who you thought could not be overridden.

God told Joshua that no matter how large the Canaanites towered over them or how deep the Hittites growled, that no man would be able to stand before Joshua to block him from getting where God said Joshua was going to go. God knows how to handle the people who are in the way if He can just get you to walk on the property. That doesn't mean to disrespect people or to dishonor them; it just means you do not need to be intimidated by them. There is only one God, and they are not Him. While man may have a say, he does not have the final say. While your boss may have a thought, your boss does not have the final thought. While the people opposing you may have a word, it is never the last word—unless you let it be the last word because you stop walking in faith.

Stay Tied to God's Word

Joshua's predecessor, Moses, was never considered a military man. He was a prophet and a leader. However, Joshua—who was now in charge of leading the Israelites into the Promised Land—had more of a military approach about him. He was one of the two men who had wanted to go into the Promised Land forty years earlier and take on all the inhabitants. Joshua was a fighter. He was a strategist. As a strategist, Joshua had plans on how to approach the enemy, invade their territory, and take over the land. Yet God made it clear to Joshua before Joshua ever took one step toward his destination that this battle was God's. And since it was God's, it would be fought, and won, His way.

> This book of the law shall not depart from your mouth, but you shall
> meditate on it day and night, so that you may be careful to do according
> to all that is written in it; for then you will make your way prosperous,
> and then you will have success. Have I not commanded you? Be strong

and courageous! Do not tremble or be dismayed, for the LORD your God is with you wherever you go. (Joshua 1:8–9)

Before the battle even began, God reminded Joshua to stay tied to His Word. He reminded Joshua that strength was found in God's presence with Joshua and not in Joshua's plans. God reminded Joshua that it was God himself who would make Joshua's way prosperous and grant him success, not Joshua's strategies. As a military man, Joshua would have wanted to come up with his own methods on how his dispatch of men should take the land. He would have wanted to lean on his own understanding, but God reminded Joshua that the way to experience success in the new land he was about to enter was by keeping himself tied securely to both the presence of God and His Word.

> *The only guarantee of success is when you seek God's way— when you seek God.*

God's prescription for success is no different for us today. It has been spelled out for us clearly in that we are to stay within the boundaries of His instruction. This is because God's ways are not our ways and God's thoughts are not our thoughts. The only guarantee of success is when you seek God's way—when you seek God. In 2 Chronicles 26:5 we read God's prescription for success as revealed in the life of Uzziah: "He continued to seek God in the days of Zechariah, who had understanding through the vision of God; and as long as he sought the LORD, God prospered him." Uzziah experienced a life of success while he sought God and His ways. However, not too long after this verse, Uzziah's heart swelled with pride in his success and he turned away from God's ways. It was then that Uzziah was "cut off from the house of the LORD" (2 Chronicles 26:21) and lived out his remaining days as a leper.

Living a successful life as a child of the King is not rocket science, men. God doesn't hide the path toward living out your destiny in some obscure location tucked away in some well-guarded vault in the Amazon. It boils down to seeking the will and ways of the King. It's not much different than what you would find in an earthly kingdom.

The nature of a kingdom assumes a king. It assumes a ruler. The nature of a king assumes he rules. The more God is in the ruler role in your life, the more you will see Him opening doors. And you will know that it is God opening the doors because He will do things that you didn't even know He was going to do. Or He will do what you asked Him to do, but He will do it in a way that you never expected. While God's precepts and principles are predictable, God's ways are unpredictable. God says,

> For *as* the heavens are higher than the earth,
> so are My ways higher than your ways
> and My thoughts than your thoughts.
> For as the rain and the snow come down from heaven,
> and do not return there without watering the earth
> and making it bear and sprout,
> and furnishing seed to the sower and bread to the eater;
> so will My word be which goes forth from My mouth;
> it will not return to Me empty,
> without accomplishing what I desire,
> and without succeeding *in the matter* for which I sent it. (Isaiah 55:9–11)

God will accomplish His purposes, but He will often do it in a manner unlike what you or I or Joshua would have strategized. In fact, sometimes God's ways can seem downright strange. He has a million ways that He can use to accomplish the same thing. Don't even try to figure Him out because not only will you not be able to predict Him, but also you will not be able to outwit Him. Just let Him lead. I know it is difficult for men to let someone else lead, but He is God, after all. Success comes when you master the skill of following God well.

Consider the strategy God gave to Joshua for how to take the city of Jericho once he had crossed into the Promised Land. No military leader throughout all of history would have come up with a strategy that involved marching his entire army out in the open, vulnerable to attack, around the city once every day for six days. Then, if that wasn't enough, God told Joshua to march this same army around the city on the seventh day, seven times. When the priests made a long blast on the ram's horns at the end of the seventh time, all of the people in the army were told to shout. And that was it. That was the strategy.

I wish I could have seen the look on Joshua's face when he was told about that strategy. But what is even more intriguing is that God never asked Joshua to use this same strategy again. It was one approach to take one city. And thankfully Joshua was wise enough to realize it. Joshua didn't say, "Well, it worked last time, so let's use it on all of the cities we need to conquer." Joshua understood that he needed to keep his eyes on God to know what his next steps should be.

Men, let go of the past, seize your spiritual inheritance, focus on God rather than people, and tether your decisions to His Word. Even if that means marching around a city every day for seven days. Because it is then that you will claim the victory that includes living out the fullness of your destiny. It is then that you will experience kingdom rule and authority on earth.

PART III

THE FUNCTION OF A KINGDOM MAN
(PSALM 128)

A kingdom man is a man who visibly demonstrates the comprehensive rule of God underneath the Lordship of Jesus Christ in every area of his life.

12

A KINGDOM MAN AND
HIS PERSONAL LIFE

If you are a messed up man, you are going to contribute to a messed up family. If you are a messed up family, you are going to contribute to a messed up church. If you are a messed up church, you are going to contribute to a messed up community. If you are a messed up community, you are going to contribute to a messed up state. If you are a messed up state, you are going to contribute to a messed up country. And if you are a messed up country, you are going to contribute to a messed up world.

Therefore, the only way to have a better world made up of better countries composed of better states filled with better communities influenced by better churches inhabited by better families is by becoming a better man.

It starts with you.

The path to a better world begins with you. And me. It begins with us.

You become a better man by aligning yourself under the comprehensive rule of God over every area of your life—under God's kingdom agenda. You do it through choosing not just to be a man, but also a *kingdom* man. By being the man that David wrote about in what has become my benchmark passage for manhood, Psalm 128. No other passage in Scripture so comprehensively covers the kingdom impact of a kingdom man through all four spheres of life, which include the personal, family, church, and community. Psalm 128 is specifically written to men to tell them how they are to function.

It is the mantra of a kingdom man:

"How blessed is everyone who fears the LORD,
Who walks in His ways.
When you shall eat of the fruit of your hands,
You will be happy and it will be well with you.
Your wife shall be like a fruitful vine within your house,
Your children like olive plants
Around your table.
Behold, for thus shall the man be blessed
Who fears the LORD.
The LORD bless you from Zion,
And may you see the prosperity of Jerusalem all the days of your life.
Indeed, may you see your children's children.
Peace be upon Israel!" (Psalm 128)

In this Psalm, David outlines the life of a kingdom man. He begins with the *personal* life of a man who fears the Lord: "How blessed is everyone who fears the LORD, who walks in His ways. When you shall eat of the fruit of your hands, you will be happy and it will be well with you."

Then he moves to the *family* life of a kingdom man: "Your wife shall be like a fruitful vine within your house, your children like olive plants around your table."

> *David covers all of the components of a kingdom man in Psalm 128.*

Next, David talks about the kingdom man in relation to the *church*: "The LORD bless you from Zion."

And ultimately David concludes with the kingdom man and his *community*, including his greater society and his legacy: "And may you see the prosperity of Jerusalem all the days of your life. Indeed, may you see your children's children. Peace be upon Israel."

In this one compact yet comprehensive passage, David covers all of the components of a kingdom man in Psalm 128. First and foremost, the blessing comes when a kingdom man fears the Lord and walks in His ways in his personal life.

It Starts with You

The greatest example I have ever seen of a kingdom man is my father.

In a day and age, as well as in a struggling community in urban Baltimore, when so many men were leaving their wives or leaving their families, my dad never did. Despite a rocky and tumultuous marriage for the entire first decade, my dad didn't budge. Despite economic challenges, layoffs, and little work that made it nearly impossible at times to feed a family of six, my dad remained constant. Despite working as a longshoreman without all of the advancements in technology we have today and under the weight of backbreaking labor day in and day out, my dad never missed a day when there was available work.

And when there wasn't work to be done because of the nature of being a longshoreman in the '50s and '60s, my dad still provided for his family without hesitation. At times, these periods without work could last as long as three months. Yet in those periods, I never once saw my dad sitting idle. Neither did he send my mom out to get a job. Rather, he provided for us by hiring himself out for odd jobs and projects he could do in a makeshift shop in our basement. And to make sure that we always had enough to eat, he went fishing. My dad would literally go fish for our meals off bridges, catching herring by the hundreds with a net.

We ate herring for breakfast, herring for lunch, herring for dinner, and herring for dessert. In fact, we ate herring so much that to this day I don't like to eat fish anymore. I've had my fill of fish. Despite how I feel about fish, I have never forgotten my father's consistency in providing for our family in spite of the challenges that he faced as a black man in urban America in the middle of the twentieth century. Taking care of his family was his priority. Something he did at all costs to himself.

Even though I grew up without much, I never once remember wondering whether there would be anything to eat, whether we would have heat, or whether I would have the clothes and shoes that I needed to go to school. I never heard my dad complain. And I never heard my dad blame anyone else for the obstacles he faced. My dad loved, and still loves, my mother in such a way that wasn't expressed only in words, but also was expressed in his actions. With both of my parents now over 80 years old, it is still common to see them walking around holding hands. My mother loves to tell the story about the time a woman came up to them as they were walking out of a store and said, "You two must not be married."

My mom replied, "We are married. Why do you say that?"

The lady replied, "Because you're holding hands."

Both of my parents laughed and told her that they had been married for over sixty years and still loved to hold hands.

My father is a kingdom man who fears God.

Sometimes when I was growing up, I would wake up around midnight because I heard a noise downstairs, so I would go check out what the noise had been. It would be my father on his knees praying fervently for our family. No matter how tired he was, even if he worked six days a week, he would spend that time in the late hours of the night praying for his family on his knees. It is a priority that he passed on to me. He covered each of us by name with specific prayers. He covered my mom as well while kneeling at the throne of God. My dad believed that prayer was not simply an exercise to do before a meal, but that prayer was a joint venture with God. It was a tool to bring heaven into history.

I never heard my dad blame anyone else for the obstacles he faced.

Not only that, but my dad also made a point to always know where each of us was, where we were going, who we were going with, and when we would be home. He wanted to know because he wanted to approve first and he wanted to hold us accountable. His intentional involvement with each of his four children set a standard within us to work as hard as we could to better our lives and to take responsibility for the care of those under us.

My dad always tried to instill in us a long-range view of life. He always tried to point out that God had something bigger in store for us beyond the immediate accomplishments of where we were at that time in our development. For example, my brother Arthur was an impressive athlete in high school. He was captain of the high school football team and was the Maryland state high school unlimited wrestling champion, weighing in at 215 pounds. Despite Arthur's athletic successes, he struggled academically. His struggle was actually due to boredom, in that he needed someone to help him to find his path in life through his giftedness in sports. His school counselor recommended that my parents consider placing him in special education classes. Others encouraged him just to try and finish high school; then go to trade school to equip himself to make enough money to get by.

While there is nothing wrong with going to trade school if that is the best you can do at the time, my dad would always tell my brother not to listen to the people who told him that. He told Arthur not to believe what they said because he told him that whatever he lacked in academics, God could make it up somehow if Arthur would just commit himself to it, trust in the Lord, and try. My dad always encouraged us to do the best we could with what we had and leave the rest in God's hands.

Because of my dad's encouragement, Arthur applied to college and got a football scholarship to attend Delaware State College (DSC). At DSC, Arthur was inspired by various professors to apply himself and improve his academic performance. Later, Arthur was accepted at Kansas State University to work on his master's degree in sociology. Following that, he received an academic fellowship enabling him in the doctoral program. Today he holds the rank of full professor at Florida Atlantic University, where he has also served as Chairman of the Sociology department and Director of Ethnic Studies.

When I used to visit Dr. Arthur Evans in Florida, I would be ushered up ornamentally positioned steps into a private office replete with an atmosphere of distinction and honor, all because Arthur had a father, who despite being dog-tired and having to work his fingers to the bone just to feed his family herring understood that his son had a future beyond what anyone else told him he had and beyond what even he could see.

The Blessing of Fearing God

One of the most important principles my father modeled for me was his adherence to the kingdom. On a daily basis, I saw him honoring the specific order in which God had arranged things for the operation of His kingdom principles to work. If more men would abide by this kingdom order, the world in which we live would be drastically different. Politics would be graphically changed, and every segment of life would be lived out from a position of clarity rather than confusion.

Our lives would be, as we read in Psalm 128, *blessed*.

I want to briefly revisit the concept of blessing before going deeper into this benchmark Psalm. In Scripture, a blessing refers to the favor and goodness of God that has been designed to flow to you and through you. The latter part of that definition is the most critical to remember simply because many people limit the blessings they receive by failing to comprehend the biblical principle of a blessing. The moment a blessing stops with you, it cancels the furtherance of a blessing because a blessing is intended to go through you to others. Paul wrote in Acts 20:35, "Remember the words of the Lord Jesus, that He Himself said, 'It is more blessed to give than to receive.' "

Essentially, if you allow yourself to be a conduit rather than a cul-de-sac for a blessing, you become a mechanism that God blesses and uses to bless others. In

> *A blessing refers to the favor and goodness of God that has been designed to flow to you and through you.*

fact, when you go to God in prayer concerning something that you need Him to do to, with, or for you, make it a point to let God know how what you are asking for will also flow through you to others. Let Him know that you recognize that the benefit coming to you will also be beneficial to someone else. Otherwise, based on the principle of kingdom giving, you are actually limiting yourself from receiving a blessing, as described in Luke 6:38: "Give, and it will be given to you. They will pour into your lap a good measure—pressed down, shaken together, *and* running over. For by your standard of measure it will be measured to you in return."

Whatever you want God to do for you, make sure you are seeking to pass that very thing on to someone else. That is the formula that has been outlined for us in reference to being blessed.

Psalm 128 tells you that you will be blessed if you fear the Lord and walk in His ways. The Hebrew word *yare* that we translate into the English word *fear* combines the concepts of both dread and awe. Mixing the two together equates to taking God seriously by coming under His rule in such a way that you hold Him in the highest esteem.

We live in a day of the casual Christian where many men seem to be politely Christian by acknowledging God, but not necessarily taking Him seriously. This is similar to how we may think of a police officer on the highway. When the police car is not on the highway, many of us drive without a strong awareness of how fast we are going. As long as we are staying on track with the majority of the cars, we assume we are going the speed limit. Yet as soon as we spot the police car on the side of the highway or coming up behind us, our eyes immediately shift to the speedometer no matter what we are doing. Our right foot immediately shifts from the gas pedal to the brake. I'll admit it, mine does. This is because the police officer's presence has greatly affected us. Our hearts might even start to beat faster while our palms get sweatier if the police officer decides to drive directly behind us. And some of us will even slow down below the speed limit, just in case.

Yet when that policeman decides to exit off the ramp, it is back to business as usual for most of us. The thing we need to keep in mind with God, though, is that not only is He omnipresent—meaning that He is everywhere at all times—He is also omniscient, meaning that He knows everything at all times as well. God isn't just around when you are at church, doing your devotions, or praying. Living in the fear of God involves a mind-set that acknowledges His continual presence and that He ought to be taken seriously, especially in light of the reality that your life's blessings are tied to fearing Him and holding Him in the highest esteem.

Men, that truth ought to affect what you do when no one else is looking. It ought to affect how you plan the use of your time and money, what you say, how you treat your family or your wife when no one else is around, how you conduct your business practices and the diligence with which you do your work, and the thoughts that you entertain. To fear God means to acknowledge Him as Lord over your life and align your actions, words, and thoughts accordingly.

Too many of us want God on sale. We want a discount God. Just like the discount stores are often more packed than the high-end stores, people want God, but they only want Him cheap. The moment He starts to come at full price, we are not sure we want Him anymore. The moment He starts to actually cost us something, we rethink whether we want Him at all. In essence, we marginalize God, keeping Him on the outskirts of our lives. Like He's a spare tire, we want Him near only in case things go flat.

The Concept of Fearing God

Yet situated at the end of the Old Testament is the book of Malachi, which is infrequently used for devotionals or sermon subjects. But it is a book that speaks directly to the concept of fearing God. Malachi isn't one of those feel-good books of the Bible. It is not one that will get you pumped up and excited as you start your day. In fact, if you read through Malachi long enough, what God has to say through his prophet just might irritate you.

Malachi is packed full of God telling His people, the Israelites, like it is. He was telling them then, and us today, that He wants, desires, and demands that we take Him seriously. That we give Him the fear, honor, and respect that is due to Him.

At the very beginning of Malachi, God laid out what it means and does not mean to fear Him in one of the most critical oracles in Scripture pertaining to living as a kingdom man. He said:

> "'A son honors *his* father, and a servant his master. Then if I am a father, where is My honor? And if I am a master, where is My respect?' says the LORD of hosts to you, O priests who despise My name. But you say, 'How have we despised Your name?' *You* are presenting defiled food upon My altar. But you say, 'How have we defiled You?' In that you say, 'The table of the LORD is to be despised.' But when you present the blind for sacrifice, is it not evil? And when you present the lame and sick, is it not evil? Why not offer it to your governor? Would he be pleased with you? Or would he receive you kindly?" says the LORD of hosts. "But now will you not entreat God's favor that He may be gracious to us? With such an offering on your part, will He receive any of you kindly?" says the Lord of hosts. (Malachi 1:6–9)

God began by telling the Israelites that while they called Him father and master, they did not give Him the honor or the respect that a father or a master should be given. In fact, God said that it was not simply that they were not giving Him honor or respect, but that they even despised Him. He said that they despised His name.

God referenced His name frequently throughout Scripture and even more frequently in Malachi. However, when God talked about His name, He was not referring to the nomenclature, but rather to what His name reflects and represents—His person and His position. When God said to the Israelites at the time of Malachi, and to us today, that they despised His name, He was saying that they were not recognizing the uniqueness of His personhood or His position. He was saying that they were not holding His name at the level that His name represents.

To fear God simply means to take God seriously, as opposed to taking God casually.

A good way to bring this principle to light is through electricity. When we turn on our lights, use our appliances, or plug our computers into an outlet, we benefit from electricity. Electricity is good. In fact, life would be a lot more difficult if we did not have electricity. We need, want, and enjoy electricity.

But the thing you ought to always remember about electricity is that you should never play with it. Don't go stick a screwdriver into an outlet just to see what might happen. That's not how you want to interact with electricity. That's not how you want to use the name called *electricity*—because while that name is a blessing, if used improperly, it can hurt you. Not because electricity is trying to be mean, but because electricity needs to be respected. If you choose to play with it, then the thing that was designed to bless you, benefit you, help and support you can destroy you. Not because it wants to destroy you, but because when it is not handled rightly, it hurts.

> *To fear God simply means to take God seriously, as opposed to taking God casually.*

To fear God is to take His name—His position and His person—seriously.

Don't misunderstand me. You have probably sung the song that says, "I am a friend of God." And God really is your friend. But in being your friend, He does not stop being your God. Those of you who have children probably understand what I am talking about. You probably know the fine line between being a parent and being a friend. In fact, I hope you are your child's friend—*kind of.* In other words, I hope you are your child's friend up to a point. But I hope you never erase the line between parent and child.

We have too many parents today who are too buddy-buddy with their kids. The reason you know they are too buddy-buddy is because the child no longer respects the parent's position. As a result, we have chaos, disorder, disrespect, and damage in the home.

God wants to be your friend.

But more than that, He demands to be your God.

Fearing God First

God began His talk in Malachi by reminding the Israelites that they called Him father but that there was no honor and respect for whom He is and the position that He holds. He wanted them to remember that He is not just some running buddy. He is a great King.

The Israelites, like a child will do at times, played dumb and asked Him how they were defiling Him. After all, they went to the tabernacle. They offered their sacrifices. They paid their dues.

Yet God pointed out that what they were giving Him was their leftovers. They were not giving Him their best. Instead, they were giving Him the things that they could not use. They were bringing lambs that couldn't see and couldn't walk. Basically, they were bringing Him their junk.

Men, you don't have to curse God openly to despise Him. All you need to do is tell Him that you don't think much of Him by giving Him your leftovers.

Think about it this way. Let's say you get a call at work on Friday. The person on the other end is a representative from the White House. The scheduling secretary on the line tells you that the President and his wife are coming to your town and that they have decided to eat dinner with a local family on this trip. They have chosen your home to host them. The President of the United States has chosen to have dinner with you.

> *Men, you don't have to curse God openly to despise Him.*

Immediately, you call home to your wife to tell her the great news. You start listing a few things that you could serve the President and his wife for dinner—maybe you could grill some filet mignon or bake some fresh salmon. But your wife tells you that you don't need to worry about it because she has plenty of leftovers in the refrigerator from this week, and she assures you that they will still be good by the time the President and his wife arrive.

Your wife reminds you of the fried chicken you ate as a family not too long ago. She thinks there is enough left over to serve at least one, or both, of the First Family. She offers to combine that with some leftover lasagna from Monday as well, to offer a variety. She also reminds you of the leftover green bean salad, since neither you nor the kids seemed to eat that much of it on Wednesday night. There is plenty, she assures you, for dinner.

You would quickly reply, "I love you, Honey, but are you out of your ever-living mind? This is the President of the United States. We aren't going to serve him leftovers."

And while that response may seem like a no-brainer to you, what many men do is offer up to the Lord of Hosts, the King of the Universe, their leftovers and then wonder why God doesn't like hanging out with them. Many men give God their leftovers and then question why He isn't blessing them.

There are multiple ways that we bring our leftovers to God and demonstrate to Him that we do not fear Him or His name. One of the ways is when we give God our leftover time. This is when we give God our attention only after we are finished watching all of our shows, when our schedule has nothing else left on it, or if we are not too tired.

Another way we give God our leftovers is when we give Him leftover service. We throw something together when it comes to doing something for Him. But when it comes to doing something for us, we want it to be done exactly right. This is like a waiter who comes to your table smacking gum and neglecting to bring menus to you. Later on when you are eating, the waiter comes to clear away your plates even though you are not done. But since he has gotten tired of waiting for you to finish, he goes ahead and grabs your plates. Then when it is time to leave, he still wants you to give him a tip. Most likely, you would not leave him even a small tip. Why? Because it was lousy service. It was leftover service.

But in Malachi 1:9, we read, " 'But now will you not entreat God's favor that He may be gracious to us?' " Even with lousy and leftover service, God says, "You are asking for a tip? You are asking for my favor, blessing, and grace?"

A third way we give God our leftovers is when we give Him our leftover money. We give Him what is left over after we have purchased, financed, or secured all that we want for ourselves. This is when we look to God to help us pay our bills, bless us, get us a raise, get us out of debt—but give Him only our leftover money.

Suppose you went to work this week and on Friday your boss came out and said, "Here is $10 because that is all we have to pay you this week. We spent the rest of it already." How do you think you would respond to that? I doubt you would respond with great enthusiasm. Because you didn't work hard all week just to get some leftovers. You view yourself as worth a lot more than $10. But that is exactly what we do to God when we give Him our leftovers. That is why God calls our giving in Scripture the *first fruits* because He wants us to give to Him first out of honor and respect for who He is.

God says that you don't have to openly despise Him to despise Him. All you have to do is give Him your leftovers while at the same time asking Him to bless you. All you need to do is bring leftover praise, leftover worship, leftover love, or leftover time while asking Him to do exceeding abundantly more than you could ask or think.

That's called despising or failing to fear God.

Your Attention, Please

Fearing God is more than about simply checking off a list.

It is an attitude that shows up in everything and everywhere—similar to what happens every Sunday during football season. Seventy thousand or more people show up for a monster "worship service" each Sunday—and even more than that tune in for the live streaming. I call it a "worship service" because worship is simply paying homage to the object that you are worshipping. It means giving both honor and respect.

Now, on paper, this is just a one-hour service. Every football game is only sixty minutes. But this is an interesting one-hour service because only seventeen minutes of activity occur in this one-hour service. This is because the clock keeps running while the players are either in the huddle, coming out of the huddle, or in between plays. When you boil it down, the actual time of play for this service is approximately seventeen minutes.

Yet so dedicated and so reverent are those who have come to worship on this Sunday, that they don't mind that seventeen minutes of activity have been turned into a one-hour service, which actually translates into a three-hour experience. And even if a football game goes into overtime, not a soul is going to complain that the service went too long.

They don't grumble about the breaks in between the quarters or about half-time. They don't even complain that they have to spend the extra time funneling in with thousands of other people on crowded interstates to get a parking spot. In the heat, snow, or ice, you don't hear anyone mumbling and fussing that they have to walk such a long way to get to the service. Instead, excitement is on their faces and anticipation is in the air. Likewise, when the service is over some three hours later, there will be another hour or two to walk to the car, get out of the parking lot, and drive home. On top of that, you will never hear anyone complain about how much they "put in the plate" for a ticket or any additional contributions they made at the concession stand.

Essentially, seventeen minutes of action that translates into a sixty-minute service that becomes a three-hour experience will take nearly seven hours from most men who want to attend it. Yet you don't hear anyone complain that it requires seven hours out of their day, that the service is too far away, that there is a problem parking there, that there are too many people who go there, and that the sanctuary is too big.

Instead, they want more. Because on the way home, they will turn on the sports radio to hear the sports announcers talk about what they just saw. And after the men get home, they will turn on ESPN or the NFL Network to watch clips of what they just saw. Not only that, but also the next morning they are going to open up the sports section to review what they had just seen. In other words, they are going to review the passage from the "service" the day before.

Even if a football game goes into overtime, not a soul is going to complain that the service went too long.

And to prepare for the next week, they are going to listen to the same sports radio, or television networks, or read the sports sections in the paper—and possibly even add some fantasy football in there.

In other words, the football team of their choice will have taken over. Which leads me to just one question: What has your football team done for you lately?

Football teams are notoriously hit and miss. Sometimes it's a touchdown. Sometimes it's an interception. And yet giving them the respect and honor that exudes from an attitude and atmosphere of dedication doesn't seem like too much of a stretch for most people. Yet God—who does not hit and miss, but who is faithful, consistent, and great, as well as a provider and worthy of our worship—can often barely get some attention during grace before a meal.

Maybe if God were speaking through Malachi today, He would have said it differently. Instead of comparing our gifts to Him versus what we give our governor, He would have compared how much time, attention, money, and respect we give Him versus what we give our favorite sports team. Either way—or whether you choose to fill in the blank with whatever grabs your attention and demands your respect—the comparison is eye opening.

In God's kingdom rule, living in fear of Him means taking Him seriously by letting your actions reflect your honor and respect for Him.

According to Psalm 128, God clearly says that, if you will fear Him, you will benefit in three areas: your *fortune, feelings,* and your *future.* By functioning first as an individual under the rule of God, He says, "You shall eat of the fruit of your hands." In other words, you will have the capacity to enjoy the benefits of your labor—your *fortune.*

Following that, we read, "You will be happy," which refers to your *feelings.* Happiness is an emotion that often depends upon circumstances. God says that if

> *God says that if you fear Him and walk in His ways, the circumstances surrounding the fruit of your hands will produce happiness.*

you fear Him and walk in His ways, the circumstances surrounding the fruit of your hands will produce happiness. And last, He says, "It will be well with you." That statement references your *future*—it *will be,* not just *it is.* The man who fears the Lord by functioning under His covering with his actions and his heart can expect to receive the blessings outlined in Psalm 128.

It is important to note that a kingdom man begins with knowing that you must make a personal response to God that nobody else can make for you. Remember, the definition of a kingdom man is a male who visibly demonstrates the comprehensive rule of God underneath the Lordship of Jesus Christ in every area of his life. As a kingdom man, you must take God seriously. It starts with you. Everything else—family, church, community, and even our society—is predicated on how the individual governs himself under God. We can't expect to have order, stability, and peace around us until we have it within us.

Fearing God with Your Feet

Shortly before Jesus completed His earthly ministry on the cross, He made a foreshadowing statement to His disciples (see Matthew 16:21–23). He let them know that He was about to suffer and die. However, Peter would have nothing of it. He argued with Jesus and protested against what He had just said. Yet Christ confronted Peter by pointing out that Peter was no longer thinking and functioning like a kingdom man. Peter was not setting his "mind on God's interests, but man's" (Matthew 16:23). Because Peter was not acting or thinking like a kingdom man, Jesus even addressed him as "Satan" and a "stumbling block."

To get Peter back on track, Jesus took the next few moments to set the path of personal discipleship straight, not only for Peter and all of His disciples, but for us as well.

> Then Jesus said, "If anyone wishes to come after Me, he must deny himself, and take up his cross and follow Me. For whoever wishes to save his life will lose it; but whoever loses his life for My sake will find it." (Matthew 16:24–25)

The Greek word for *life* that Jesus chose to communicate with was *psuché*, which literally means the vital force of life, a living soul.[2] When Jesus spoke of saving or losing your life, He chose the word meaning soul. Your soul is you. It is the core of who you are, as well as what makes you different from anyone else around you. Your soul is not your frame or your body; rather, it is your capacity to feel, think, choose, and desire. It is your essence—the part of you that will continue beyond time into eternity.

Jesus told us as His disciples that if we want to stick with Him and follow Him—if we want to save our soul—it will require three things. First, we will need to say *no* to ourselves—to deny ourselves. This is because your biggest problem is not outside you; your biggest problem is inside you. In fact, your biggest problem *is* you. To follow Christ means you need to learn how to say *no* to you. This is a big deal because *you* don't like *you* to tell *you* no. At least not about what *you* want. It's easy enough for me to say *no* to myself when it comes to eating squash. But when it comes to eating fried chicken, that is a whole different story. That is when I run into a soul temper-tantrum trying anything and everything to talk me out of saying no to myself.

Yet to fear God as King and follow Christ as Head, you must deny yourself. Then, you must take up your cross—which is a frequently misunderstood concept. Often I will hear people quoting this passage in relation to a difficult situation at work, at home, or in their personal life. I will hear things like, "I'll just have to put up with that person and pick up my cross" or "My in-law is just the cross that I must bear" or "I have a headache so that must be my cross." But what Christ said is that you are to pick up *your* cross. The cross that you are bearing is *you*. There is only one reason why the Roman government ordered someone to carry his own cross and that was because he was going to be crucified on it. A cross is an instrument of death. When Jesus carried His cross, He was walking to Calvary with the instrument of His own death. Carrying His cross was an open and tangible submission to the law of the land, the Roman government.

When a believer denies himself and carries his cross, he is submitting to another law higher than himself. He is yielding himself to what God has asked of him—which is to deny his wants, desires, and will in exchange for following the wants, desire, and will of the One he is following. Even in the garden before Jesus carried His cross, He said to God, "Father, if You are willing, remove this cup from Me." Jesus didn't want to do it. Yet He also said, "Not My will but Yours be done" (Luke 22:42). To carry your cross, men, is to yield your will to God's. And this must be done on a daily basis (see Luke 9:23).

Last, Jesus said that after you deny yourself and carry your cross, you are to follow Him. Keep in mind where Jesus just told His disciples that He was going—to the cross. He just told them that He was going to suffer and die. One of the reasons that we as men are not ruling our personal lives—our *psuché*—is because the thing that is supposed to die is still alive.

Paul illustrated this reality clearly when he wrote the following to the Romans:

> Therefore I urge you, brethren, by the mercies of God, to present your bodies a living and holy sacrifice, acceptable to God, *which is* your spiritual service of worship. And do not be conformed to this world, but be transformed by the renewing of your mind, so that you may prove what the will of God is, that which is good and acceptable and perfect. (Romans 12:1-2)

In the Old Testament times, a sacrifice was typically an animal that was killed and placed on the altar. But Paul said that as saints living in the church age, we are to present ourselves as a living sacrifice. Essentially that means that we are to be a living dead thing. To be a living dead thing involves dying to your will, wants, and desires while being fully alive to God's will, wants, and desires. Ultimately, it means placing His kingdom rule as the preeminent and solitary purpose in your life—which is exactly what Christ said to the disciples. When you deny yourself, take up your cross, and follow Him, you die while you simultaneously truly live. That is when you experience the reality that "whoever loses his life for my sake will find it" (Matthew 16:25).

What some men call life isn't really living. Only in following Jesus do you get to embrace true life.

When Everyone Is Watching

While I was going through seminary, I worked at a Trailways bus station loading buses. I worked on the dead man's shift from eleven at night until seven in the morning. When I came to work there, I realized that the guys had a scam going. A guy would punch out for lunch then have his friends punch him back in when in reality he was asleep on the job. Each man would get his turn, and the others would cover for him, awaiting their turn to get three hours of sleep while on the job. Put simply, what they were doing was stealing. The men had agreed to work for eight hours but were stealing a few of those hours each night.

After I had been around a few days, one of the men came to ask me which part of the night shift I wanted to take for my long break. He explained the system to me, how long I could take, and whom I was to punch in. When I told him that I couldn't do it because of what God says about stealing, what I thought would be a great witnessing opportunity didn't go over too well.

Instead, the men decided to teach me a lesson.

Rather than satisfy my need for rest . . . I kept my commitment to Jesus Christ.

When buses would show up during the night to be unloaded then loaded again, the other men wouldn't show up to help. So I found myself loading and unloading buses by myself. That situation was hard. Rather than satisfy my need for rest and to have approval from my peers, I kept my commitment to Jesus Christ and honored His kingdom rule and His Word. But it ended up being painful in two ways. First, it was painful emotionally knowing that people were against me, and second, it was painful physically simply because it was a lot of work. To top it off, after all of that work, I still had to go to class during the day.

About six months into this cycle, I got called into the office. The supervisor said, "Unbeknownst to the night crew, we have had various night supervisors come down and observe the activities. We are aware of the scam. We are also aware that you have not participated in the scam, nor have you been supported when the buses came in. Because of this, we want to offer you the job of supervisor for the night shift, and we will double your pay."

Fearing God led to a blessing. My enemies became my footstool. Men, God is watching. Some of the greatness comes in history. Most of it comes in eternity. Yet if you want to be great—if you want to be blessed—take advantage of every opportunity to demonstrate that you fear God both with internal opportunities and external opportunities, holding Him in highest honor and esteem in every aspect of your life. Sometimes that will hurt. In fact, most times that will hurt at some level. But the King rewards those who fear Him, as we saw so clearly in Psalm 128, making it the foundational principle for life as a kingdom man.

One place fearing God will take you—I can guarantee—is where you will experience the blessing of the abundant life that Christ has promised you. Your destiny will be full.

13

A KINGDOM MAN AND HIS FAMILY LIFE

After writing about a man's personal life in Psalm 128, David moved to a man's family life. Verse 3 says, "Your wife shall be like a fruitful vine within your house, your children like olive plants around your table. Behold, for thus shall the man be blessed who fears the LORD."

A man's decision to marry a woman and begin a family is one the most important decisions he will ever make. Although marriage frequently doesn't, it ought to come only under the condition of great thought and readiness. I have two daughters, both of whom are married. When it came time for my daughters to get married, their future husbands had to do a lot more than just ask me for permission to marry them. These were my princesses, and I wasn't about to hand them over to just anyone.

In fact, part of the process of winning an Evans woman involved writing me a detailed and lengthy letter stating everything that he would be responsible to do and be as a husband. I told these men that I wanted it in writing just in case I ever got old and lost my memory. Seriously though, I did ask both Jerry and Jessie for a letter. And I do have them filed away just in case I ever need to remind them what they committed to do. Marriage is no small thing and should be entered into only when both parties fully comprehend both the meaning and purpose of it. When a man is a successful husband and father, he not only brings blessing into his own life, but it enables those around him to fulfill their divine destinies as well.

Psalm 128 moves first from the individual to the family, which represents the divine order of creation. As we looked at earlier, God created Adam first and gave him the responsibility of personal governance and guidelines before giving Eve to him. Adam had to first learn and establish his individual authority before expanding it to a family. Another important element to note is that David progresses to the family in Psalm 128 before he writes about the church and the community. This is because before God ever created church or civil government, He created the institution of the family.

There are very few problems in our culture today that you cannot trace directly back to the breakdown of the family. If the family functions according to God's kingdom principles, because the individuals within it are functioning according to God's kingdom principles, then it follows that both the church and society will function reflectively.

> *The goal of the family, then, is the replication of the image of God.*

As we saw earlier, the creation of humankind was so man would be an image-bearer of God himself. The purpose of being fruitful and multiplying to fill the earth was not just to fill the earth with people, but it was also to fill the earth with image-bearers. The goal of the family, then, is the replication of the image of God in history rather than to simply form a happy place to call home. The purpose of children is not merely to have look-a-likes in your ancestral line, but to produce children who will reflect the image of God throughout the world.

In establishing the kingdom institution of the family, God created the expansion of His rule in history. That is precisely why Satan is trying to destroy the family. If Satan can destroy the family, he can destroy the expansion of God's kingdom rule. Whoever owns the family owns the future. The problem in legalizing gay marriages is not entirely a problem of homosexuality. The primary problem is the redefinition of the family away from its divine design. In redefining the family, Satan is attempting to set up a rival kingdom that undermines God's purpose for the home. In warping the view of manhood, Satan is doing the same thing he tried to do when he sought to have all of the baby boys killed when Jesus was born. By getting rid of the men when they were boys, he attempted to kill the future. Men, your role is critical, and Satan's primary goal is to keep you from performing it according to God's kingdom principles.

Covenant for Life

The first kingdom principle that applies to marriage, the foundation of a family, is that we are to view and treat it not as a contract, but as a covenant. The problems arise in our marriages when we adopt our culture's view of marriage as simply a means for love and happiness. While those things are important, they aren't the *most* important things a marriage is designed to produce. Marriage is a covenantal union designed by God to increase the capacity of both partners to carry out their divine purpose for advancing God's kingdom. In Malachi, we read about this covenant:

> "This is another thing you do: you cover the altar of the LORD with tears, with weeping and with groaning, because He no longer regards the offering or accepts *it with* favor from your hand. Yet you say, 'For what reason?' Because the LORD has been a witness between you and the wife of your youth, against whom you have dealt treacherously, though she is your companion and your wife by covenant." (Malachi 2:13–14)

A covenant is more than simply some form of a contractual agreement. In Scripture a divinely authored covenant is a spiritually binding relationship made between God and His people that includes certain agreements, benefits, conditions, and outcomes. Examples of these are the covenants God made with Abraham, Moses, and David, and the new covenant through Jesus Christ. Marriage is also a covenant.

Every covenant always includes three fundamental facets: transcendence, hierarchy, and ethics. Transcendence simply means that God rules above as sovereign over the covenant. He is in charge. Hierarchy represents the specific order in which the covenantal components and participants are to function. And ethics, which are the rules that govern the operation of the covenant, include three interdependent elements: rules, sanctions, and continuity.

When a marriage functions according to the components of a covenant, the blessings of the covenant are the ultimate result. However, when a marriage functions outside the components of a covenant, the negative consequences attached to the covenant will result. Because marriage is a sacred covenant and not just a social contract, it entails sanctions and continuity that have generational repercussions. A contract is a legal agreement that does not carry within it a spiritual and divine component, while a covenant engages God in relationship to His kingdom and the spiritual benefits and losses that occur because of that agreement.

When a man approaches his marriage as a covenant in fear and reverence of God, Scripture says that his wife will be like a fruitful vine. A few years ago I went with my wife, Lois, to Napa Valley, California, to drive through the vineyards and see the process of producing wine. It is fascinating. If you have ever done the same thing, then you know that a vine must do three things to be fruitful. A vine is elevated and tied to a post for it to cling to the post so it will not drag on the ground. If a vine drags on the ground, then it won't be able to absorb the sunlight.

So for a vine to produce fruit, it must first cling, which means it must be securely fastened and tied to the post for security.

> *A frustrated or controlled vine, men, will fail to produce any fruit.*

The same is true for your wife, men. For your wife to be the kingdom woman she was created to be, you must provide a place of security that is so strong and stable that she will not only be able to, but also want to, cling to you. By enabling and encouraging her to cling to you, you will keep her from clinging to something else that is not legitimately positioned to put her in a place of personal growth and nurturing.

The second thing a vine does to produce fruit is that it climbs. A fruitful vine climbs all over whatever it is clinging to. When a vine is free to climb on that which it clings to, it expands its ability to receive nourishment and grow. What many men will do out of their own insecurities or fears is try to supplant their wives from developing the skills and gifts God has uniquely given to her. Rather than having wives who feel free to climb, these men wind up with wives who feel frustrated or controlled. A frustrated or controlled vine, men, will fail to produce any fruit.

Yet when a vine is nourished and able to both cling and to climb, it then does the third thing to produce fruit: It clusters. When a vine clusters, it produces fruit that then has the extractable juice needed to ferment into wine. Men, when you operate as a kingdom man, Scripture says that your wife will cling, climb, and cluster in such a way as to produce fruit that is not only beneficial to herself and to you, but also to those within your realm.

But keep in mind that the verse specifically says, "Your wife *shall be* like a fruitful vine," rather than *is* a fruitful vine. This is because in the home, the ordained order is that it starts with you. She becomes what you name her. If you choose not to name her at all, then she will name herself and other myriad voices will vie for her attention. But if you choose to name her a kingdom woman, she *shall be* a fruitful vine. Women were created to respond. The test of a kingdom man is measured by the response of his wife. Has she been named? Is she becoming what that name declares her to be?

Being Her Savior, Sanctifier, and Satisfier

Being a kingdom husband is a responsibility. In fact, Paul told us that it is a three-fold responsibility. The first responsibility includes being your wife's savior. We read in Ephesians 5:25, "Husbands, love your wives, just as Christ also loved the church and gave himself up for her." First, a husband ought to be his wife's savior since he is to love his wife like Christ loved the church. The last time I checked, Christ loved the church to death. So if you are still alive, you aren't finished yet. Be her savior.

He is to be her savior in the sense that he sacrifices his life for her well-being, thus capturing the essence of Paul's command that husbands are to love their wives the way Christ loves the church.

In order to discover how a man is to love his wife, we need to look at how Christ loves the church. How did Christ love the church? First, "[He] gave Himself up for her" (Ephesians 5:25). That refers to a sacrifice. Jesus' sacrifice tells husbands what it means to love. We love by choice, not by feeling. As we said earlier, loving your wife today has little to do with whether you feel like being loving today. Biblical love focuses on the need of the person being loved, not necessarily on the emotions or wants of the one who is loving. It is righteously and passionately pursuing the well-being of the other, even if that comes at personal cost or sacrifice.

Along with being your wife's savior, a husband is to sanctify his wife. Ephesians 5:26 says, "So that He might sanctify her, having cleansed her by the washing of water with the word . . ." To sanctify something means to set it apart as special and unique. A man sanctifies his wife over time through discipling her and providing a place where she is safe to grow and develop into the creation God made her to be. When you married your wife, you didn't marry just her, but you also married her history. You married all of the things that she did not tell you while you were dating that have combined together to form the way she approaches life, perceives things, and struggles or self-doubts.

> When you married your wife, you didn't marry just her, but you also married her history.

Sanctification is the process of taking someone from where they are into what they ought to be. If she has never known security or never had a man provide a stable place for her, she may be hesitant to submit to you as her husband. But through sanctification, you are able to demonstrate to your wife what it means to be covered by a kingdom man—not a perfect man, but a kingdom man who has her best interests at heart and who loves her even to the point of sacrificing his own needs and wants to provide that love.

Last, a kingdom husband satisfies his wife. Paul writes, "So husbands ought also to love their own wives as their own bodies. He who loves his own wife loves himself; for no one ever hated his own flesh, but nourishes and cherishes it just as Christ also *does* the church." (Ephesians 5:28–29). Whatever you do for yourself, you ought to do for her. You are to treat her like you treat your own body. You are to think in terms of two and never in terms of one. It is in your best interest, and hers, to satisfy your wife emotionally, spiritually, and physically.

You don't have to be a scholar as the spiritual head of your home to satisfy your wife, but you do need to be intentional about leading her in spiritual growth as her pastor. Nothing will gear her to respond to your soul like getting her to respond to your spirit. If she can respond to you spiritually because you are taking spiritual responsibility, then her soul will adapt to respond to you personally. And, of course, when she responds with her soul, she will respond with her body. What men often want is their wife to respond with her body when her soul is out of sync. And so sex isn't engaging, exciting, or dynamic, and he thinks that Victoria's Secret is going to solve the problem. Victoria's Secret can't solve that. This is an issue of the soul. But you don't heal the soul by healing the soul. You heal the soul by creating spiritual oneness.

The first step in learning how to satisfy your wife is in understanding her. Study her. Get to know her. Find out what makes her tick, what motivates her, and what inspires her. Discover what her dreams are and how they connect with your own. So many men neglect the greatest gift they have been given in life—their wife—and they do it to their own detriment. Scripture even tells us that if you do not live as a kingdom husband, even your prayers will be hindered. "You husbands in the same way, live with *your wives* in an understanding way, as with someone weaker, since she is a woman; and show her honor as a fellow heir of the grace of life, so that your prayers will not be hindered" (1 Peter 3:7).

A wife who has been given the environment to flourish as a fruitful vine first flourishes within the home. Yet as we see in Proverbs 31, she does much outside of the home as well. She is a businesswoman negotiating with merchants from afar. She has a real-estate license because she is buying and selling property. She has her own ministry looking after the poor. And to top it off, she takes care of herself, making sure she looks good and dressing in purple—the couture garments of the day. Her children are not lacking, and her husband is praised in the gates because everything she does outside of the home complements the priority of the home.

One thing that you can do as a husband to give your wife the best environment in which to flourish is to be intentional about complimenting her. Let her know on a daily basis that she is valued—and why. A woman has unique insight and perception, so just telling her that she has value to you will probably not be enough to satisfy her need to be cherished. She wants to know what it is about her that you value—what is it that is special within her that you enjoy and appreciate.

Beyond that, and what I hope every man is already doing, pray regularly with your wife. Pray with her each and every day. Pray about what is on her mind, but also pray for her. Let her hear you praying for her every day, and give her the added security in knowing that you are seeking God on her behalf and on behalf of your union in marriage.

Olive Plants

When you fear the Lord and walk in His ways, and when your wife is a fruitful vine in your home, your children will be like "olive plants around your table"

(Psalm 128:3). They won't be olive trees because an olive tree typically takes fifteen or more years to fully develop, but they will be olive plants responding to what you give them.

The interesting thing about an olive plant is that, if it is nurtured correctly, it will then become an olive tree that can produce olives for over 2,000 years. When I was in Israel at the garden of Gethsemane, I saw 2,000-year-old olive trees still producing olives because their roots run deep. As a kingdom man, one of the greatest things you can offer your children is modeling yourself as an olive tree with deep roots of stability.

My mother and father still live in the same house that I grew up in. The area was a working class neighborhood before, but now it has devolved into such a place that police cameras are on every corner to catch the drug deals going on. One time I was sitting on the porch with my kids while we were visiting and a policeman caught a drug deal going on down the street. The policeman wound up chasing the perpetrator right into my parents' front yard, jumping on him, knocking him to the ground, and holding a gun to his head. My kids and I sat there watching the whole thing go down. In fact, the last time I was visiting my parents, while I was driving through their neighborhood, I came across an entire SWAT team of about ten police officers getting ready to make a raid just as the sun was about to come up.

When I mentioned to my dad later that they might want to move now since he is in his 80s and the neighborhood isn't exactly what it used to be, he replied that he wanted to stay because that was his home. Those were his roots. He told me that God has taken care of him this long and that God would see him through. My dad is rooted. His roots are not just in a location, though. They are in God. In all the years that my father has been a believer in Christ, I have never once seen him waiver from the Word of God. His roots run deep, modeling for me a life of fruitfulness, which in turn models for my children and grandchildren how to become an olive tree.

Our problem today is not merely a lost generation, but it is the product of a lost generation. We have fathers who never saw their own fathers be a kingdom husband or a kingdom dad. So we have children raising themselves. Or we have children looking to the government to raise them. So our tables have no olive plants around them.

Our tables sit empty.

The way God designed a family to be led, particularly by a father, is around the table. A Jewish father raised his family around the table. The table was not just a place for eating. It was a place for nurturing. Food was simply the context for discipleship and relationship building. When a Jewish father sat around the table, he wasn't just filling his stomach. He was convening his family there to lead them. It was there that he led the family in devotions. It was there that he heard of any potential behavior concerns. It was there that he handed out work responsibilities within the home and checked on whether the duties had been completed. It was there that the family discussed educational issues and established strategies toward achieving goals. It was around the table that he learned what peer groups his children were associating with and what information they were putting into their minds. It was there that he poured value and significance into the lives of his children by listening to them and being with them consistently.

A Jewish family didn't sit at the table just to eat. Rather, that was a place for a man to spend substantive time every day teaching, listening, knowing, and leading his family. There were other times for these things to occur as well, but those times were always in addition to the family table. This is because fruitful vines and olive plants need consistent nurturing to produce or to grow. Yet so many of our tables sit empty today. Men's schedules are full. Women's schedules are full. Children's schedules are full. In failing to prioritize the consistency of the family table—or daily family time wherever you may choose to spend it—we have failed to lead our families well. As a result, we have a generation of young people who set their consciences to the culture rather than to that which was given to them at the table.

Despite a heavy schedule at the church, a national ministry, and traveling to preach, I have always made the family table a mainstay in our home. It was the place, when my children were growing up, where we met not only to eat, but also to engage each other according to the need of the moment. In fact, every Sunday we have two services at the church where I pastor and it is a tradition in between services for whichever members of my family are in town to gather at a table at the church to enjoy a meal together. Every Sunday you will find me there—usually with a grandchild or two on my lap—talking about the sermon for the day, talking about their lives, and investing in each other. And the first Sunday of every month, for as long as the kids have been grown, we reconvene as a family for food, devotions, fellowship, and to hear the grandchildren recite Scripture verses.

Men, do not neglect the table. Whether breakfast, lunch, dinner, or all of the above, the table is designed not merely for food, but for a connection to take place and for you to intentionally and regularly engage with those you have been destined to care for and lead well.

Future Men

Yet even beyond the table, men, it is important that you intentionally make yourself a consistent part of the family. So many men simply pop in on special occasions and then consume themselves with their work, which leaves their wives' and children's hearts left empty. Nothing can fill the hole made from the absence of a husband or father. Even the best mother in the world cannot meet the need that children have for the approval and attention of their father.

The time you spend together doesn't have to be fancy and it doesn't have to be formal, just make it a priority to be with your family. No matter how busy my schedule was, I would regularly play games with the kids while they were growing up. Several times each week I would get down on the floor—depending on their ages—and play with them. I also made it a priority to be the one who drove all four kids to school every day. It might not seem like a big deal, but when you put your children ahead of your own schedule or needs, it says a lot to them about their value. I had a full calendar, and my children knew that, but they also knew that they came first. The first thing that I did each day was load them up—after breakfast together—and take them to school. It gave us extra time together that I wouldn't have had if I had asked them to ride the bus.

Even though I intentionally spent a large amount of time with my family when the kids were younger, my greatest regret to this day is that I did not spend more. If I could do it again, I would double that time—at a minimum. It goes by so fast, means so much, and produces dividends both relationally and spiritually for generations to come.

Men, the time you spend with your family should never be a second thought. It should always be your first thought. Put first things first. If you haven't done it in the past, it is never too late to start today.

If your kids have moved out, visit them, invite them over, and call them. Or pick up the phone when they call you. One thing my wife, children, and grandchildren all know is that no matter how busy I am—no matter what time of day it is—if one of them is calling me, I will pick up. Family must come first after God. It is how He designed our lives to function. And when we function according to the principles of His covenantal and transcendent rule, not only are we blessed, but also those within our realm find themselves fruitful and blessed as they become what they were destined to be.

In the biblical culture, men didn't have to be prodded or encouraged to spend time with their families or children. They knew it was their responsibility to pass the covenantal rights and responsibilities to the next generation. In fact, men were often both the dominant presence and the dominant influence among all of the family members. However, today this role has flipped. Because of the large number of women in influential positions throughout the development of the lives of children—whether in the home, schools, or churches—most boys spend the largest part of

> *The time you spend with your family should never be a second thought. It should always be your first thought.*

their lives with women. First, in his mother's womb. Next, the babysitters are typically female, as are the nursery workers. And even most of the elementary school and Sunday school teachers are usually female. And while we praise God for the role that females play in our culture and in the church, what is frequently missing in the development of kingdom men is a strong and consistent male presence.

When you have an increase in males missing in action in culture, there is an overarching weakening of manhood felt throughout. And because of this, we are at a greater risk of raising the next generation of boys who will grow up to be men just like their mothers. Never underestimate your role as a father. Remember, Dads, that your children's view of God will largely be dependent on their view of you.

14

A KINGDOM MAN AND HIS CHURCH LIFE

Psalm 128 moves from the individual man fearing the Lord to the results showing up in his family. When the man is in alignment under God, the results of a man's relationship with God spread outwardly. Which is exactly what happens next as we continue our look at this kingdom motif. Psalm 128:5 says, "The LORD bless you from Zion."

Men, you are to receive a blessing in relation to your connection with Zion, which today is the established New Testament church. To the degree that you are not connected to Zion is the degree to which this blessing will be withheld, not only from your life, but also from those under your care.

One of my classes in seminary brought me great discouragement. In it, I had to write a paper. I always took my assignments seriously and committed myself to making an A on them. I spared no research effort, no dedication, and no time and energy to be certain that I would get an A. However, when I got my paper back, there was a big, red F written on the top of it. Not only did I not make an A, I didn't make a B, C, or D either. Boldly proclaimed for all eyes to see was my F. You can imagine how I felt, especially because of the time I had spent on it studying the original languages and researching.

Yet when I looked more closely at my paper, I discovered the reason for my F. Down toward the bottom written in smaller letters was a note from the professor. He wrote, "Tony, great scholarship. Great detail. Magnificent effort. But you answered the wrong question." All of my work addressed the wrong thing. It wasn't that I hadn't been sincere, but I had just been sincerely wrong.

The problem that we face in the church today is not that we are not sincere; it is that we have misunderstood the kingdom. The church is focusing on the wrong assignment. By misunderstanding the nature and purpose of God's kingdom, we have marginalized the church's authority and influence both within its walls and outside them.

The nature of God's kingdom on earth is not some ethereal ideology meant to play out at a later date and location. Rather, it is a biblical mandate to be relevant to the spiritual and sociological needs in today's church and society. When the church fails to function from this kingdom perspective, the church has stopped *being* the biblical church it was designed to be. The church does not exist solely for programs, projects, preaching, and buildings; rather, it exists as the primary vehicle for preparing believers to display God's glory, impact the culture, restore lives, and advance the kingdom.

The primary purpose of the church, in view of the distinctions of the kingdom, is to reveal the ethical, political, social, and economical aspects of God's rule in societies. The church is to operate in the world while offering an alternative to the world. In doing so, it sets itself apart as a haven, much like an embassy.

An embassy is a sovereign territory on foreign soil where the rules and laws of the nation the embassy represents apply. Embassies never belong to the countries that they are in. They belong to the country where they are from. If you were to visit another country as an American citizen and you went to the American Embassy, you would find that all American laws and procedures would be carried out there, no matter what country you were in. The American Embassy is fundamentally a little bit of America a long way from home.

The church is supposed to be a little bit of heaven a long way from home. It is to be the place where the values of eternity are made manifest in history—the place where the victories in heaven bear fruit on earth. It is also the place from which God commands His blessing (see Psalm 133:3) and, as a result, opens the gateway to societal transformation and productivity. Because of this and more, the church ought to be nothing less than a central component in a kingdom man's life.

My Father and Church

This might be difficult to imagine since my dad is over eighty years old, but you can still find him in the pulpit at a small Brethren Assembly church in Baltimore every Sunday morning preaching to the congregation. It might take him a few minutes to walk to the pulpit from the piano bench where he sits to lead worship, but he eventually gets there and delivers the Word. Now, he won't go so far as to ever call himself a "pastor"; he just says that he is "serving the Lord." Yet in Arthur Evans' home, church is a central point today, and it has been a central point since his conversion in 1959.

As a child growing up under his leadership, I remember that I would practically need to be hospitalized to get out of going to church on a Sunday. As a kid, I didn't like the service as much as I liked getting to run across the street afterward to buy some candy from the local store. I looked forward more to that than to getting dressed up and sitting in a pew.

> *By the time I was in high school, my dad's biblical worldview had become my own.*

Even though I wasn't at the point in my own spiritual development to benefit from the service as much as my father, his consistency in embracing the role of the church in his life set the example for doing so in my own life as I grew older. In fact, by the time I was in high school, my dad's biblical worldview had become my own. At times I would walk over four miles just to go to church on Wednesday nights when he wasn't able to get off work to drive me. And, yes, sometimes that was even in the cold Baltimore snow.

Not only did my family and mentors play a large role in helping me to avoid common pitfalls that many young men fall into, but the church proved to be an important element as well, which is what it means when God blesses you from Zion.

God Bless You from Zion

What is Zion? A number of references in Scripture point to this place called Zion. There was a mountain called Zion, which served as a holy place where God's presence was found. There was also a city called Zion, the City of David or Jerusalem, where God dwelled. The temple in the Old Testament culture was also referred to as Zion. It was the gathering place where a father would take his family to worship *Yahweh*, as well as to offer sacrifices. It was inconceivable that a Jewish mother would have to wake up a Jewish father to ask him if he was going to Zion today.

Everything centered on this temple called Zion. It was the permanent location of what had been a temporary dwelling, the tabernacle. When the Israelites convened at Zion, they were reminded that they were part of a covenant and a people who think alike, act alike, and view life alike. It was a covenantal community all sharing the same value system because they all lived under the same King and belonged to the same kingdom.

In Psalm 128:1, we saw how God blesses you if you feared Him. Yet in Psalm 128:5, we read that God will also "bless you from Zion." As a believer, God is going to do certain things simply because of your relationship with Him, but He will also do certain things because of your attachment to Zion. These things emanate out of your connection with others in the midst of His corporate presence.

As an individual, you can experience God's power and His blessing up to a certain level. However, some aspects of experiencing both you will never see individually. These aspects only come as you are connected to His people. It is similar to a family. There are some things that each family member will experience on his or her own. But other things, like a family vacation, only occur as a result of being connected to the group. In the Old Testament Zion, the man took his family and those under his care to Zion because he knew that was where each of them would receive favor and direction from God. It was where the principles and promises of the covenant were transferred. Zion was where he connected his family to something bigger than themselves—to a part of a community of people who thought and functioned under God's kingdom covenant.

When you are part of something larger than yourself, you will get more out of your experience with God.

One of the things that we, as men, have often missed in the church in multiple ways is both experiencing and displaying God's power and blessings collectively. With all of the emphasis on autonomy and individualism, it is easy to forget God's collective program as well as the implications of being disconnected in an intentional, participatory manner, as opposed to merely something you show up to do in order to check it off of your list.

Keep in mind that you are not an only child. Jesus taught the disciples to pray,

"*Our* Father who is in heaven" (Matthew 6:9), not "*My* Father who is in heaven." When you are part of something larger than yourself, you will get more out of your experience with God and His blessings in your life by connecting with His people for His purposes than you will on your own.

That is why the writer of Hebrews made the point that we as a body should continually seek to convene: "Not forsaking our own assembling together, as is the habit of some, but encouraging *one another* and all the more as you see the day drawing near" (Hebrews 10:25). We have not been instructed to assemble together simply for the purpose of getting together. It is for a purpose far greater than that. It is in connection with the "day drawing near." In connection with how we, as the church, are to participate in God's kingdom.

It is in this same book of Hebrews where we read about the contemporary nature of Zion as the established church whose head is Jesus Christ. Hebrews 12:18–24 says,

> For you have not come to *a mountain* that can be touched and to a blazing
> fire, and to darkness and gloom and whirlwind, and to the blast of a
> trumpet and the sound of words which *sound was such that* those who
> heard begged that no further word be spoken to them. For they could not
> bear the command, "IF EVEN A BEAST TOUCHES THE MOUN-
> TAIN, IT WILL BE STONED." And so terrible was the sight, *that* Moses
> said, "I AM FULL OF FEAR and trembling." But you have come to
> Mount Zion and to the city of the living God, the heavenly Jerusalem, and
> to myriads of angels, to the general assembly and church of the firstborn
> who are enrolled in heaven, and to God, the Judge of all, and to the spirits
> of *the* righteous made perfect, and to Jesus, the mediator of a new covenant,
> and to the sprinkled blood, which speaks better than *the blood* of Abel.

Just as the Old Testament Israelites were part of a covenant, we are part of a new covenant. Ephesians tells us that when the church of Ephesus gathered, they were to come together as one without any barriers between them because of their foundation of Christ.

> So then you are no longer strangers and aliens, but you are fellow citizens
> with the saints, and are of God's household, having been built on the

foundation of the apostles and prophets, Christ Jesus Himself being the corner *stone*, in whom the whole building, being fitted together, is growing into a holy temple in the Lord, in whom you also are being built together into a dwelling of God in the Spirit. (Ephesians 2:19–22)

Just as Satan seeks to break up the family in an effort to destroy the future, he also wants to break up the community of believers because he knows that an anemic church will never experience the presence of God. The greatest deterrent to solving the problems facing our nation today is the division of the body of Christ. In terms of cultural presence, influence, and community impact, we have failed to make any noticeable dent because of the fractures and isolation that exist between us.

God is a God of unity, and where there is disunity and division, His Spirit is not free to dwell. Our corporate experience with God in making a difference in our land is muted and limited to the same degree that our fellowship with one another is muted and limited. The church was not merely designed as a place for people to go once a week and feel good about a sermon or a song, but it was also created to serve as a functioning community where the gifts, talents, and skills of all members are grafted into a greater and more productive whole.

Refocusing the Church

Far too many men in the church are like teenagers living in a house. They want their own room, their own television, their own iPod, their own iPad, and their own phone, and then they want to shut and lock their own door. But later they will come out and ask, "What's for dinner?" In other words, they want convenience when it comes to the corporate dwelling, but they do not want to be disturbed with anything else. Many men have come to view the church for its convenience—help me, bless me, serve me, preach to me, sing to me, pray for me, but don't expect me to be a vehicle to minister to anyone else or join with you to impact the world.

Because our churches have often been more focused on building buildings and creating programs than about advancing the kingdom in personal lives, families, communities, and our nation by leveraging the talents of those within it, many men have come to view the church as a task to be *done* rather than a community to be *in*.

Or, worse yet, some men view church like a prostate exam—something that can save your life but is so unpleasant and invasive that they want to put it off for another day.

While the church frequently does a good job providing many avenues for women to participate, it seems as though we have produced an atmosphere for men in which they do not often feel comfortable. For example, anyone who knows me knows that I love hot weather. I live in Texas, and my favorite months are in the summer. In fact, sometimes I will even drive around in the summer in Texas with my windows rolled down and the air-conditioning turned off. I love the heat. But Lois likes it cold. That's why in the evenings we often battle it out at the thermostat for how warm or cold the house is going to be to sleep in. We go back and forth on the setting because we respond to two different things from a temperature standpoint.

> *Many men have come to view the church for its convenience—help me, bless me, serve me.*

In most lives, albeit exceptions always exist, women were built to respond to relationships while men were built to respond to ruling. Women were wired to respond to cuddling, while men were wired to respond to conquering. We are made differently so we respond differently. Yet what frequently happens in the church is that the church will call for relationships without giving men an opportunity to rule. Or the church will offer nice, warm fuzzies to cuddle emotionally with while withholding or ignoring any potential challenge that men can conquer. Often the temperature in the church is set for women, and therefore, men sit there cold.

So many men come to church only because they are pushed to do so or because they feel guilty for not doing so. They stand there as the music plays with a feeling that something just doesn't seem like it fits. Kind of how I would feel if Lois ever asked me to hold her purse. Something just doesn't seem manly about church for many men. It's cute with pretty decorations, soft music, long songs, and an atmosphere often geared toward evoking emotions—which is why a lot of men simply do their time, albeit sincerely, rather than view it as a vehicle through which they are to change the world.

Yet that wasn't the church Jesus established. When Jesus talked about His body, He spoke of a force that even the gates of hell could not prevail against (see Matthew 16:18). *Ekklésia,* or church,[1] in the New Testament Greek societies referred to a governing counsel who legislated on behalf of the population. It didn't refer to a place where you went to simply get inspired. Rather, it was where men came together to fulfill legislative duties.[2]

Somewhere between the cross and contemporary culture, the concept of *ekklésia* has gotten watered down from the full potency of its original meaning. To be a part of the *ekklésia* was to be a participant in the governing body tasked to bring heaven's point of view into hell's society. The church is intended to be *a group of people who have been called to bring the governance of God into the relevant application and practice of humankind.*

> *When Jesus talked about His body, He spoke of a force that even the gates of hell could not prevail against.*

When Jesus spoke of the church withstanding the forces of the gates of hell, He chose the term *gates* because at that time a gate referred to a place where legislative activities took place. The gate was where the leaders of the town would meet to enact business and make decisions on behalf of the community.[3]

The concept of legislation for the body of Christ is reinforced by the fact that Christ gives "keys" to the church so those to whom they have been given can use them to gain access to heaven's authority and execute it on earth (see Matthew 16:19). While Jesus is positioned at the right hand of God to govern from heaven, we are also positioned with Him (Ephesians 2:6), which reveals why God will often choose what He is going to do based on the church (Ephesians 3:10).

The purpose of the church reaches beyond a mere meeting place for spiritual inspiration or analysis of the culture in which it resides. The purpose of the church, *ekklésia,* is to manifest the values of heaven within the conflicts of humankind. In fact, one of the ministries that we have in our church involves mediation where lawyers will meet with those who are in conflict in an effort to find a resolution. This weekly ministry is available to anyone in need; it is one of the many ways we have organized the church to try to meet the real and relevant needs of people.

The Assembly Line

Today, many of our churches have strayed from their purpose as heaven's embassy on earth, having become more akin to a club. As a result, we are facing a cultural tsunami that is sweeping away a generation of men and boys from becoming the kingdom men God intended them to be. The church, like an assembly line, has been designed to produce something: kingdom men—visible, verbal, unapologetic disciples of Jesus Christ. When an assembly line does not produce what it is supposed to produce, we can conclude that there is a flaw in the factory. A design issue must be addressed. When you look at the weakness of Christian men in particular today, we must also conclude that there is a flaw in the factory that has been established to produce them.

The goal of the church is to transmit a biblical worldview so men begin to think and function from a theocentric perspective rather than a homeocentric perspective. Each church ought to make one of its primary priorities as having a men's ministry that seeks to instruct, inspire, encourage, equip, and hold accountable its men to become kingdom men. Each church ought to focus heavily on discipleship. Discipleship is a *developmental process of the local church that brings Christians from spiritual infancy to spiritual maturity so they are then able to repeat the process with someone else.*

Discipleship in the church should be designed to enable men to overcome the illegitimate influences and definitions of manhood that they have been accustomed to or influenced by. When a man faces obstacles and challenges in his quest to live as a kingdom man, the support system for facing those obstacles victoriously that God has placed on earth is the local church. It has been the rare man, in my experience, whom I have seen fully take advantage of what the church has to offer. Life is not to be lived as a lone ranger. That would be similar to putting the starting quarterback on the line at the beginning of the football game and facing him off against eleven other players—alone—while telling him to overcome that obstacle.

Oneness in the body of Christ—whether racially, generationally, or within relationships among men—is a requirement to advance the kingdom simply because of the nature of the body as the apostle Paul described it. We are a body with multiple parts that performs multiple functions. And unless you are intentionally connected to and operating in the mind-set of a body, you will fail to maximize the purpose and strategic presence of the church.

One of the church's primary roles is to create an environment for men that fosters authentic discipleship. And one of your primary responsibilities, men, is to locate a church body that you can be a part of that offers discipleship opportunities, sound teaching, small groups to connect with, and ways for you to serve. If you put more thought in choosing what car you last purchased than in choosing the church you are a part of, men, you have shrunk from your responsibility as a man, not only personally, but also for your family.

Even though a man's involvement with the church is so critical, it seems that in most churches, men are not taking an active role in any men's ministry or in transferring a kingdom worldview. What is missing on the assembly line, the *ekklésia,* is the sense that one of the main reasons the church is here is the production of spiritually strong men. The church must be where a man is not only to receive instruction for his own personal growth, but also where he is to take that instruction and teaching and rehearse it with his family during the week. It is supposed to be the place to grow boys into men through spiritual parenting such as what Paul wrote to his own "true children" and "beloved son" in his letters to Timothy and to Titus (see 1 Timothy 1:2; 2 Timothy 1:2; Titus 1:4).

> *One of the church's primary roles is to create an environment for men that fosters authentic discipleship.*

In these letters, Paul was writing to men who were taking over pastoral responsibilities. While he was careful to tell them about preaching, teaching, and serving, he also talked to them about spiritual mentoring. In the same way that parents should be raising their children to become responsible adults, the church exists to provide a parenting environment to grow God's children up to be spiritually mature and responsible as well.

Spiritual Fatherhood

When Paul wrote to his son in the ministry, Timothy was a reasonably young pastor in his mid thirties or early forties. Timothy served, to use our contemporary nomenclature, as the senior pastor at Ephesus Bible Fellowship. His church is the one church that is written about more than any other church in the New Testament. Three chapters in Acts, the book of Ephesians, and the first church addressed in Revelation are some places that focus on Timothy's church.

When my wife, Lois, and I walked through Ephesus together among the archeological ruins, we were able to see the library along with both the houses of the elite and of the commoners. Even the town market in the commercial district of the city was there for us to get a glimpse of how things used to be. One of the things that stood out to me the most was that the church at Ephesus was founded during a time of great idolatry. Among many temples, the Temple of Diana was there in the midst of a very pagan community.

This was the backdrop when Paul planted a church, positioning his son in the faith, Timothy, as the pastor. When Paul wrote to Timothy to advise his disciple on how he should pastor such a young flock in the middle of such a volatile culture, Paul wrote,

> I am writing these things to you, hoping to come to you before long; but in case I am delayed, *I write* so that you will know how one ought to conduct himself in the household of God, which is the church of the living God, the pillar and support of the truth. (1 Timothy 3:14–15).

Paul made sure early on that Timothy didn't go to the marketplace to get his instructions on how to run his church. He didn't conduct an opinion poll or borrow from the culture. Paul made it clear that the church was supposed to function in light of its position as "the pillar and support of the truth." This is because the job of the church is to hold up the standard of truth. It is not to satisfy the culture or even to make everyone feel good. It is to offer God's truth in a world without it.

What is missing for men in the church are spiritual fathers like the apostle Paul. Without spiritual fathers to set the thermometer, we have an assembly line turning out a feminized version of what it means to be a man and calling him "nice" and "helpful" rather than "strong" and "responsible." Even though Timothy and Titus were not Paul's biological children, he spoke to them and related to them as a father would to a son. In turn Timothy was to call the men to lead in public prayer, as well as to equip and identify men under him to serve in the leadership in the church (see 1 Timothy 2:1–3). Timothy *had* a father in Paul and was to *be* a father to those under him.

It is bad enough if a young man does not have a biological father to mentor him and help him grow, but when there is no spiritual father as well, he is fatherless twice. When a boy or a man is fatherless twice, he doubly misses out on receiving the blessing that he needs in his life.

> *The job of the church is to hold up the standard of truth.*

All throughout biblical history, a boy looked forward to receiving a blessing. The blessing was when the father would put his hands on his son and transfer the benefits of the father's life to the next generation. A blessing always meant speaking the future into someone. Unfortunately, what is prevalent in the church today is that we have a generation of unblessed men. And because we have a generation of unblessed men, we have a generation of men who are not able or willing to pass on the blessing themselves simply because they have not been taught the pillar of truth—God's Word—in such a way that they have learned to make it real in their own lives. A sermon on Sunday isn't enough to make disciples, no matter how great the preacher is.

Put the Word to Work

The Word of God is not simply meant to be known, but it is also meant to be applied. When Jesus mentored his disciples, He did it in such a way that He imparted the truth in action. Discipleship always includes information, but discipleship is not complete until it also includes emulation. Every man is to have a spiritual father who guides his life in the ways of God, and every man is to be a spiritual father to someone whom they influence as well. You should both *have* a spiritual father and *be* a spiritual father. Without this connection, church is simply something to do rather than a means through which your life changes and impacts others. Along with spiritual fathers, a man also needs brothers. A real brother walks with you when the world walks on you.

The one thing that Jesus did with the men that He led was that He kept putting them in challenging situations. He didn't just spend all day teaching the Bible or leading them in worship songs. Rather, He allowed them to be in challenging scenarios where their faith was tested and they were required to man up. He put them in places where to move forward they had to *move*. They had to take a step of faith. In fact, Jesus was so radical in how He led that He actually got men to leave their nets—their way of life—to follow Him. Many of the disciples dropped their nets to follow Jesus; we can hardly get men to drop their remotes to follow Him today. And then we wonder why we are not seeing more of heaven on earth and why our wives are not supportive or willing to submit.

Jesus was the consummate mentor. A spiritual mentor disciples those within his realm in such a way that advancing God's kingdom becomes a reality. Sometimes that is done in the context of teaching. But often it is done in the context of modeling. A kingdom man is to live in such a way that the next generation says, "I want that. I want what you have." He is to model kingdom living in his actions and in his relationships with others. Mentoring is not some formal thing you do once a week for an hour; mentoring is a way of life.

Yet not only are we missing many of these men as mentors for the kingdom of God to show younger men how they are to be, but also so many young ladies are being raised without a kingdom man in their life, so women don't even know what to look for in a man to marry. A man's intentional and strategic involvement in his local church must be a priority both to give to others and to learn from others.

The assignment of the church is to instruct and model for men how to reclaim their divinely ordained roles not just in the society, but also in the church. The biblical church exists to advance God's kingdom, not just to defend it. Unless the church purposefully sets out to become kingdom-minded, we are not being the church. Rather, we are being a club or a social group based on a certain moral code of conduct and belief system. Yet no club or social group ever changed the face of a society. If we are going to impact our communities and our nation for Christ, we are going to need to be the church that Christ established. Our seminaries are going to need to start teaching their students more about advancing the kingdom than about how to *do* church. And our spiritual leaders are going to have to start modeling oneness for a kingdom agenda outside of church walls rather than autonomy and their own agenda within them.

Make the Change

Men, get involved. Get connected. Serve. Lead. Mentor. Pray. Teach. Train. Discover how God has gifted you and how those gifts can benefit the church. Are you great at fixing cars? Then consider starting a workshop where you train disadvantaged youth through your church to acquire the skills they need to get work and get off the streets. Do you have a background in law? Then start or participate in a ministry within the church that moderates disputes according to biblical principles of reconciliation. Do you know the ins and outs of computers? Reach out to others in the church or in the community who can benefit from your expertise. Are you a successful businessman? Then mentor the young adults in your church, or in the community through your church, through allowing them to shadow you at work or spend time with you in your realm. The possibilities are endless. And the outcomes are priceless.

In fact, each man doing his part is how most battles are won. It is how the Israelites defeated the Amalekites, for example. Exodus 17:11–12 tells us,

> So it came about when Moses held his hand up, that Israel prevailed, and when he let his hand down, Amalek prevailed. But Moses' hands were heavy. Then they took a stone and put it under him, and he sat on it; and Aaron and Hur supported his hands, one on one side and one on the other.

Moses held up his hands during the battle to invoke heaven's assistance in earth's conflict. Because the battle waged on, Moses' arms got tired. He wanted to quit. He wanted to give up. Yet because Moses had other men who were able to come alongside of him when he was worn out, together they made sure that heaven came down on behalf of earth. And since they did, Joshua beat the Amalekites in the battle. What determined the outcome in the valley were the men on the mountain. Just like a football game is never won or lost by one man, the victory over the Amalekites came as a result of men coming together in their respective roles to be stronger as a whole than they could ever be on their own.

I look forward to the day when earth's battles are being won and God's kingdom is being advanced because men link with men to call heaven down to earth. When that happens, the church will have a visible impact, not only in the lives of the members and their families, but also in their community, our nation, and our world.

Many Christians today are spiritual orphans—children of God with no family relationship. Others are like foster children, bouncing from house to house to house, never finding a home. Yet we all know that children develop best in families. They develop best when they are connected.

If you are a disconnected Christian man, you are living outside of God's blessing. When a man either neglects or abandons his local church, he limits the favor or blessing that God wants to bring to him, as well as through him to his family. As a result, it will not only take him much longer to arrive at his destiny, but it will hinder his family's progress in arriving at theirs as well.

I am sure that most of you are familiar with what is called the HOV (high-occupancy vehicle) lane. The HOV lane is on the side of the highway dedicated solely for those not traveling alone. If you are ever traveling alone in the HOV lane, a police officer will pull you over and give you a ticket. The lane has been set aside only for the use of vehicles with more than one occupant. If someone is not with you, then you need to get in the traffic and the mess just like the masses. Yet if someone is traveling with you, you get to take the private route bypassing the masses unhindered and unblocked—getting you where you need to go faster than the rest of traffic would have allowed.

Men, God has a special lane for those of you who intentionally link yourself with others in the body of Christ. It is a lane that will allow you to go farther and faster in His kingdom than you ever could on your own. It is His *ekklésia*, His church.

15

A KINGDOM MAN AND HIS COMMUNITY LIFE

No one pays for a ticket and parking to go to a football game just to watch the huddle. The huddle does nothing in and of itself. The purpose of the huddle is to plan how to score. Then you have to show what you can do as a team when eleven men on the other side of the ball are daring you to go public with your private conversation.

Church is the huddle, men. What we do after the huddle, in our community and in our nation, reveals the true strength of our team. A community ought to be a better place than it was before, if the men in it are acting as kingdom men. The world ought to feel our impact, for good. The absence of kingdom men in Abraham's time led to a deteriorated society in Sodom and Gomorrah. Homosexuality had become the norm. Terrorism ran rampant in the streets as people threatened and carried out both murder and rape. This was a time of oppression, inequity, injustice, and economic instability. In many ways, it was a time similar to our own.

Lot's failure to live as a kingdom man in an already downtrodden community led to the downfall of his family and added to the demise of everyone else. If Abraham could have found just ten good men who lived there, the cities would have been saved (see Genesis 18:32). But he couldn't. What's worse, neither could God.

A country will know when men are being kingdom men in their homes and in the church. As we have seen, Psalm 128 begins with the foundation of the personal life, moves to the family, then goes to the church, and concludes with the community and the nation. Psalm 128:5–6 finishes with, "And may you see the prosperity of Jerusalem all the days of your life. Indeed, may you see your children's children. Peace be upon Israel!"

Unless we address the man problem in our country, we will not survive. No government program or initiative will work to save our culture and our nation if men will not rise up to become kingdom men first in their own lives, in their homes, in their churches, and in their communities. No amount of money will fix the problems that we are facing as a nation. And definitely no amount of legislation will fix what is ultimately a spiritual problem of men being out of alignment with the Lord God.

When Men Are Missing in Action

The end of a story is always more important than the start. People will frequently flip to the last page, last chapter, or the conclusion of a book to read it before starting at the beginning. This is because they want to know if it ends well or if the end is compelling. They don't want to waste their time on something that doesn't end well.

A good friend of mine recently told me that he got a copy of one of my books, and since it was so long, he went straight to the conclusion. The conclusion grabbed him, thankfully, so he then started back at the beginning. The message moved him so that he later organized an event held for hundreds of people to come hear me talk to them about the topic of the book. That event, in turn, resulted in increased awareness about community impact and racial unity, which God then used as a critical step in strengthening our capacity for training church leaders and individuals around the country.

I'm glad the conclusion got my friend to read farther.

But sometimes the end of something isn't as great as the beginning. In that case, when an author chooses to end on a downer, there must be a reason. Which is exactly what happened in the Bible. It is what God did with the Old Testament.

The Old Testament begins with promise and hope, "In the beginning, God created . . ." Creation symbolizes life, breath, and energy. Yet the end of the Old Testament concludes with the warning of disaster. Though God said he would send another prophet to Israel, Malachi points out in the last verse in the Old Testament the idea that a nation flooded with broken father-child relationships would be a nation consumed with a curse. "He will restore the hearts of the fathers to *their* children and the hearts of the children to their fathers, so that I will not come and smite the land with a curse" (Malachi 4:6).

Once again, men, Scripture points out that we are responsible. Once again, the state of the nation depends on the state of the man. Once again, our actions, choices, and values determine the quality of life for those around us—even as far-reaching as those within the country in which we live.

The absence of men with hearts turned toward their children—and the result of that, the hearts of the children turned away from their fathers—destroys the environment for passing on the covenant and passing down the blessing. A blessing was a covenantal term for men. In biblical times, men lived for the blessing. They wanted it so badly that Jacob's story showed how much a man would do to deceive for it and Esau would seek to kill because he lost it. Because to pass down the blessing was to pass down God's covenant to the next generation.

A blessing involved divine destiny, significance, authority, and a productive future. The blessing was always tied not merely to what you were, but also to what you were destined to become. The importance of the blessing is that it told the man what he was going to be. When God sanctioned Abraham to give him the blessing and to pass on the covenant, He said of Abraham's son Isaac, "I will establish My covenant with him for an everlasting covenant for his descendants after him" (Genesis 17:19). Though Isaac received the covenant God had made with Abraham, part of the blessing also passed to Ishmael, Abraham's illegitimate son, in that he would be "fruitful and will multiply him exceedingly. He shall become the father of twelve princes, and I will make him a great nation" (Genesis 17:20).

As a result of the covenant God made with Abraham, Abraham—at ninety-nine years old—circumcised himself and all of those within his household, influencing those within his realm with a visible reminder of a future promise. A covenant signifies dominion, and dominion always reaches beyond you to bless those

> *Our actions, choices, and values determine the quality of life for those around us—even as far-reaching as those within the country in which we live.*

within your realm. Abraham didn't just pass down the covenant to Isaac, but he also passed it down to the future generations.

What many boys and men are missing today is knowledge of God's covenant promise. And so they stay stuck in who they are rather than become what they are destined to be. No one has ever told them that they are princes under the covering of a covenant. So they live an unblessed life because that is their name. This generation of boys has never been blessed because there is a generation of men that has never been blessed. So there is nothing to pass down; it's like a runner in a relay with no baton. There is nothing to pass. As a result, the country suffers under the weight of a curse.

> *The solution to reversing the curse is simple: Kingdom men, man up.*

Few people would argue that our communities and our country are feeling the continuous tremors of a curse. Yet the solution of turning that curse into a covenantal blessing doesn't come through more tax dollars, government programs, or building more prisons.

The solution to reversing the curse is simple: Kingdom men, man up.

Only when men take their rightful place within our culture as the husbands, fathers, and citizens that they were created to be then will the atmosphere radically change. A man with his heart turned toward his children assumes that this same man's heart is also turned toward his wife, since it is in the best interest of his children that a father loves the children's mother. Likewise, a man with his heart turned toward his children assumes that this same man's heart is turned toward the church and his community, since it is in the best interest of his children that these entities be functioning as God intended.

If we are going to have restored communities and a transformed nation, God's people will have to start keeping their promises. God's men are going to have to start being real men rather than simply trying to look like men on the outside.

No More Facades

People will dress the part when they bowl to make sure that they have the full experience. To look the part of a seasoned bowler, men may wear certain clothes and expensive shoes and bowl with elite balls. Yet the thing that I find amusing is that no matter how great a man looks while bowling, if his ball goes in the gutter, he hasn't done much of anything at all. He is simply a failure who looks good because the goal of bowling is knocking down the pins, not to look the part of a bowler. If the pins are still standing, he has failed.

We have a lot of fancy churches in our country with a lot of fancy-looking men attending them. We have the right architecture, the right equipment, and the right songs. We even have the right-sounding things to say. But the true test of Zion does not rest in how good Zion looks; rather, it is in what kind of impact Zion is making in the community at large.

What is important to notice about the progression of Psalm 128 is that God starts with the individual, moves to the family, moves to the church, and then moves to the society. That is how His kingdom works. His kingdom works bottom up, not top down. Yet everyone these days seems to be more concerned with what the White House is doing than what their own house is doing or what the church house is doing. When society functions according to kingdom principles, though, it parcels out the responsibilities for maintaining a healthy, functioning society into more areas than just the government.

A theological view of government is one that keeps the government small while respecting the influence of the church and home on a community. The church cannot afford to have the politics of men determining the operation of the kingdom of God. This is because God does not ride the backs of donkeys or elephants. He has His own kingdom agenda—of which government is a part—yet of which the individual, family, and church also play a large part.

Whenever the church gets dragged down and divided over political sides, we have missed the kingdom. Just as the captain of the Lord's army informed Joshua before the battle of Jericho that he hadn't come to take sides, but that he had come to take over (see Joshua 5:13–14), the body of Christ must recognize that, for community impact to occur, we need to follow God's agenda. God's kingdom purposes transcend politics, personal preferences, racial divisions, and all other agendas. Only when the citizens of the King operate by the precepts of His kingdom will we see the transformation of our culture.

Societal impact isn't determined on the basis of the health of the existing society either. In fact, the book of Jeremiah gives an example of this when God tells His people who are living in the midst of a pagan land, Babylon, that they are to "seek the welfare of the city where I have sent you into exile, and pray to the LORD on its behalf; for in its welfare you will have welfare" (Jeremiah 29:7). The Israelites were to make the city in which they lived a better place because of their

presence. It was in the welfare of that city where they would discover their own welfare; however, they were to be an integral part of improving the society while not merely complaining about it and waiting on someone else to make a difference.

> *The Israelites were to make the city in which they lived a better place because of their presence.*

The lack of kingdom men is the scourge of our day. We have already looked at the ramifications that show up in our culture such as poverty, high dropout rates, imprisonment, divorce, delinquency, crime, abuse, drug use, teen suicide, and aimlessness. When the lack of positive male influencers is the cause of so much societal deterioration, then the introduction of positive male influencers arises as the natural cure.

Mentoring the Next Generation

Tucked away in the middle of one biblical genealogy after another is a model of a mentor who impacted his community. His name is Asher. The Hebrew word *Asher* means happy one.[1] Asher was a satisfied and contented man, based on his name, who fathered four sons and one daughter. Because of his influence in the lives of those within his realm, what is recorded about Asher isn't recorded about anyone else in all of the genealogies listed before and after him. We read, "All these *were* the sons of Asher, heads of the fathers' houses, choice and mighty men of valor, heads of the princes. And the number of them enrolled by genealogy for service in war was 26,000 men" (1 Chronicles 7:40).

Asher's legacy is unique from the rest in that it says that his sons were the heads of the princes. Essentially, Asher mentored leaders who were positioned to influence the kingdom as mentors themselves. A prince is a king waiting to happen. By influencing princes, Asher's sons influenced society.

One of the greatest things that my father instilled in me as a child growing up in the middle of a country torn by racial disparity and injustice was that I was not primarily to identify myself by my ethnicity, but by my citizenry. As a citizen of heaven and a child of the King, my father always taught me to remember that I had royal blood flowing through my veins. If people called me names or didn't treat me justly, he would remind me that that wasn't a reflection of who I was—it was just a reflection of what they failed to realize, that I was a prince.

Men, a world of princes is in our nation today; they have no one to let them know it like my father did for me. There is no one to study the Bible with them, lead them to church, correct them when they are wrong, teach them about life and how to treat a girl, and what it means to be responsible and make wise decisions. What this has resulted in is a form of spiritual castration. Their royalty has been ripped from them by a culture that doesn't recognize their prince status.

What our nation needs today are men who will step up and be like Asher and his sons—men who will be "heads of the princes." If that does not happen, then we will continue to face generations of men who do not know how to conduct themselves in the kingdom of God or on this earth.

Mentoring is so essential to the development of a boy into a man, in fact, that whenever a young boy was earmarked to be a king later in life, the care of many people went into training that boy on how to be a king. Yet somewhere along the way, we have come to believe that the princes in God's kingdom don't need any significant training at all.

With the growing absence of fathers in our land—whether spiritually, physically, or emotionally—someone needs to step in as surrogate fathers to raise the next generation of men. And if we in the body of Christ don't do it, then it will be musicians, entertainers, or peers that will fill that void.

When God spoke of being a "father to the fatherless" in Psalm 68:5, He wasn't referring to some ethereal spirit floating around in never-never land. He was speaking of His people who are to be His representatives—His hands and His feet—being surrogate fathers to those in need. That's what it means when James wrote, "Pure and undefiled religion in the sight of *our* God and Father is this: to visit orphans and widows in their distress" (James 1:27).

Too frequently, we relegate only those as orphans who have experienced the death of a parent or parents while overlooking those who are spiritual orphans, or whose father has abandoned them relationally, emotionally, or physically. A child without the positive influence and presence of a father—whether that father is alive or dead—lacks a father. That is an orphan. What we need to do is open our eyes to see the multitude of orphans in front of us. On our very doorsteps are the lives of those who have been left on their own without anyone to speak life into them or to raise them. The boys in need of surrogate fathers—in need of mentors—are not just boys, but also princes.

Not only did Asher's sons influence the future generations by mentoring princes, but they—and other men like them, such as the sons of Issachar and Benjamin—were also "heads of the father's houses." Asher wasn't the only man raising up the next generation of leaders. He was one of many men who made it his goal to strengthen the nation through leading well.

Leaders Leading Well

A leader is someone who knows the way, goes the way, and shows the way. The greatest summary of a leader in Scripture is found in Ezra 7:10: "For Ezra had set his heart to study the law of the LORD and to practice *it*, and to teach *His* statutes and ordinances in Israel." Being a leader first requires personal responsibility and then responsibility to those around you. The men who were "heads of the father's houses" weren't satisfied with just living in the house and eating the food; these were men who had accepted their role to lead.

The reason it is so essential for a man to lead well as the head is not so he can dominate those around him, but so he can be a channel through which the blessing is passed. In biblical culture, the covenant was always passed down through the men. The covenantal rights, blessings, and even the curses that came from not fulfilling the covenant came through a father to his sons. Headship wasn't a title but a responsibility.

What has negatively impacted our society so much is the number of men, particularly men within Christian circles, who attempt to bully those around them—either their wife or their children—through claiming the title of head without exercising the responsibilities that come with that title such as loving, leading, and providing well. It would be similar to my saying that I want to be a preacher and receive all of the benefits that come with being a preacher, but without preaching. Or if I were to say that I want to be the senior pastor and exercise all of the authority that comes with overseeing the leadership of a church, but I don't want to come to church on Sunday. That would be blatant misuse of a title, which is what a large number of men in Christendom do today with regard to headship. As a result, our society suffers from the ramifications, and we are left with a culture in chaos.

While Asher was the only man we know about who raised men to be heads of princes, he wasn't the only man mentoring the next generation. Isaachar, Benjamin, and many others each did their part to raise "mighty men of valor"—a generation of warriors who knew how to take a stand when a stand needed to be taken. They weren't wimps, and they didn't raise wimps. They were men of courage and conviction, equipped to take risks for the right cause. They knew how to make decisions on behalf of those they defended.

> *Isaachar, Benjamin, and many others each did his part to raise "mighty men of valor."*

Today, while battles rage around the Middle East and elsewhere, an even greater battle threatens to undo us from within, and that is the deterioration of our nation's strength economically, spiritually, and socially. However, what we have often done in the body of Christ is to isolate social ministry to a select few while remaining myopic in our view of what "mighty men of valor" are to be about.

Calling All Males

Men, leading well involves loving well. It involves aligning yourself under God in such a way so that you place the best interests of those within your realm as a priority in your own life. Putting the best interest of others above your own means recognizing God's headship in fulfilling your own and modeling yourself after the greatest mentor of all—God himself. And the only way to do that is to know Him well.

Knowing God and keeping Him at the forefront of decisions, thoughts, and life was so essential in the Israelite culture that God would call all of the males out three times a year to appear before Him. This was on top of regular festivals, sacrifices, memorizing His Word, and time spent at Zion. While I touched on this passage briefly before, this request was in the middle of laying down the ground rules for the men of Israel as they related to God's covenant.

Three times a year all your males are to appear before the Lord GOD, the God of Israel. For I will drive out nations before you and enlarge your borders, and no man shall covet your land when you go up three times a year to appear before the LORD your God. (Exodus 34:23–24)

What made this instruction so peculiar was that God called all of the men of Israel to appear before Him at one time. That meant that anyone who had the sexual identity of maleness was required to attend. So that meant the men who ran the businesses, served in the military, operated the government, and basically guarded the community. It included the men who served as the teachers, doctors, and farmers. To essentially remove most, if not all, of the existing leadership from a nation would shut down banking and commerce, as well as everything else. Beyond that, it would no doubt leave a nation vulnerable to attack. There would be no police force in place and definitely no military. It was an obvious risk.

Yet so important was it for the men to appear before God as a group on a regular basis that God himself, in their absence, oversaw what the men had been charged to do. It says that God himself would "drive out nations before you and enlarge your borders, and no man shall covet your land when you go." Essentially, God held up three fingers and told the men, "You come appear before Me because I've got it."

By appearing before God in a communal fashion, the men were reminded of not only His preeminence over all things, but also His sovereignty as ruler over their lives. As we saw earlier, they were not told to simply appear before God. They were told to appear before the "LORD your God." Again, anytime you see the word LORD in small capitals in the Bible, it is putting the word God on steroids. It is referring to God's relationship with humankind as Sovereign and Ruler. We could translate that to read, "Three times a year, your men are to appear before the King—the One who is telling you what to do."

As a result, the "One who told them what to do" drove out their enemies. He drove out the things that threatened to destroy their careers, productivity, peace, homes, and communities. Not only that, but He also expanded their borders. He expanded their capacity to receive more from Him—not just for themselves, but also to impact others. God didn't have to try to figure a way to raise or cap the debt ceiling; instead He expanded the productivity of the land. In other words, He protected and expanded the nation.

It costs us a combined total of over $380 billion annually just on public assistance and lost revenue relating to what is largely a result of the misuse or neglect of biblical manhood in our country.[2] If we merely aligned ourselves as men under the sovereign rule of God, we wouldn't be facing the economic crisis that is staring us down today.

Until the men in our land join together as kingdom men under the Lord our God, we are operating out of alignment. We are doing everything that we can to drive out nations, enlarge our borders, and protect what we have from others. Yet judging by the current state of the influence of Christianity in our country, we aren't doing a very good job at all. To make an impact on the culture, as men we must recognize that we answer to the sovereign King—and we answer to Him together.

> *If we merely aligned ourselves as men under the sovereign rule of God, we wouldn't be facing the economic crisis that is staring us down today.*

Our success is largely tied to our collective spiritual subordination. We are stronger together.

A Strategy for Community Transformation

Kingdom-minded men are always about leaving a legacy of the transforming power of God for those they touch. Kingdom men never forget there is a connection between knowing God and knowing justice and between loving God and loving others.

Although the theme of God's justice and deliverance is illustrated throughout all of Scripture, the Old Testament prophets provide the greatest information on social impact. They present God's viewpoint on biblical justice, what many today have termed social justice, repeatedly tying oppression directly to society's spiritual departure from God.

For example, Israel's worship was rejected because of an absence of helping those in need in society (see Amos 5:21–24). The Israelites were taken into captivity and held in bondage because of their rebellion against God (see Ezekiel 33:10–33). In Malachi 3:5, God personally promises to judge those who oppress others—to oppress others isn't simply something that is done to them; it is also something that *is not done* for them.

Most people link the destruction of Sodom and Gomorrah to the presence of homosexuality in the land. And while that was a contributing factor, it is not what God points out as to why He destroyed them when speaking through the prophet Ezekiel. Rather He destroyed them because they were proud, indulgent, and they failed to "strengthen the hand of the poor and needy" (Ezekiel 16:49, NKJV).

God's heart is found in strengthening those in need. Jeremiah 9:24 says, " 'But let him who boasts boast of this, that he understands and knows Me, that I am the LORD who exercises lovingkindness, justice and righteousness on earth; for I delight in these things,' declares the LORD." If we know God, then we ought to be about the things He is about—which always includes helping others, especially those who need it the most. There is no greater category of those in need than the fatherless.

In helping those in need, we introduce a system, one created by God that provides a divine alternative so that the world can see what happens in a society when God is followed as ruler. Behind every physical problem is a spiritual problem. By reaching out to decaying communities in the name of Jesus Christ, we are addressing the underlying spiritual issues rather than just the temporary physical issues, thus allowing for an opportunity for long-term solutions. Social ministry must encompass the spiritual and the physical. Only then will true impact occur.

> *Social ministry must encompass the spiritual and the physical. Only then will true impact occur.*

Because of our ability to provide this spiritual perspective on the challenges facing us as a nation, we as men acting on behalf of the church are the ideal group for meeting the needs of our society—particularly in relation to raising up the next generation of kingdom men. We are also ideal for pragmatic reasons. This is because within our churches, we have the physical resources necessary to carry out the action. For example, churches offer the largest, most qualified volunteer force in our nation. No group can compare with the church in terms of numbers of people available to attack the problems of our day.

Since churches exist in every community—in fact there are approximately three churches for every public school in our land—[3] the structure to address social problems already exists. We don't have to create new institutions to implement solutions, because men within the church are already within reach of every needy person in America.

Society has tried—through people, money, and programs—to save itself. Yet it continues to decline at an ever-increasing rate. The only way to make our nation whole again is if kingdom men will work together to create change. Kingdom men must infuse God back into society, because when God is dismissed from society, so are morality, decency, values, and the stability of all of our tomorrows. Removing God is akin to removing our country's immune system, causing us to suffer from spiritual AIDS and allowing cultural colds to become society's pneumonia.

No greater challenge exists today than impacting our communities and our country for good. Never before have we as a nation been at such a delicate position in so many ways. But impact is possible if men will be kingdom men. We can make a difference if we abide by the values found within the kingdom motif of Psalm 128 by being personally responsible, intentionally and strategically engaged with our families, leaders in our churches, and influencers in our community.

Time for Intervention

Closing in on four decades of ministry, I am becoming increasingly aware of the brief nature of life. None of us is guaranteed another day. And with that awareness also comes a more narrow focus—a desire to make every moment count and every choice, one that leaves behind a benefit for others.

I have had this vision for decades to see schools all across America adopted by a local church, integrating men who will then tutor, mentor, and guide the next generation. The vision began over twenty-five years ago when the superintendent of a local school approached me about the men in our church helping to quiet down gang activity and truancy and reverse poor academic achievement on the campus. As I mentioned earlier, that one school led to our church's involvement in over sixty-five public schools at this time—with additional schools calling on us to help.

But sixty-five schools aren't enough to impact a nation. Therefore, much, if not most, of my time in these latter years is focused on helping equip others to bring this vision to their community and seeking God to raise men up for the challenge. Through my national ministry, we equip leaders across the country on how to restore communities through the partnership of local churches with public schools and through meeting social needs. We do this through the National Church Adopt-A-School Initiative, which provides training and consultation to churches all across the land. Several colleges and seminaries have also begun offering this training as part of their course options because one thing that seems to be missing across the board in American Christianity is a comprehensive approach to localized community impact and transformation.

> *Last year alone, nearly one million students failed to graduate from high school.*

Without a strategy and without leveraging strengths in the body of Christ, we continue to limit our influence where it is needed the most. It is when we reconnect churches, schools, and families that we not only impact communities, but we also make a public demonstration of the strength and power of churches working together across racial, class, geographic, denominational, and even preference lines. Yet unless we choose to come together as men under the sovereign rule of our King, uniting in a common agenda, we will continue to drown in the wake of this cultural tsunami.

If annual trends have continued in America, last year alone, nearly one million students failed to graduate from high school. Over one million prisoners were high school dropouts. Over 750,000 teenage girls became pregnant. Close to one million marriages ended in divorce. All of this cost our nation over $300 billion in lost revenue, public assistance, and expenses.[4] Not to mention lost futures and lost hope. The problem in America is not just an urban problem anymore. Urban problems have reached suburban lives, threatening our already fragile economy at a price tag too costly, as well as at the cost of countless dreams.

Never before have we needed such urgent intervention.

Recently, I made a trip back to my hometown of Baltimore and walked around the campuses of my high school and junior high. Urban Baltimore has one of the lowest graduation rates in the country. As I walked around my old schools, I remembered what it was like to go to schools that were understaffed, to be taught where the teachers were overworked, supplies were lacking, and motivation to perform was dismal at best. I remember what it was like to sit in the classroom and not know how to see beyond what I could see. Sports was the only thing that mattered to many of us. When you can't see a way out of where you are, education becomes less important. In fact, when I went to college, I had to go on academic probation because my grades didn't reflect those of a good student.

While my high school grades didn't reflect that of a student with much of a future, because of mentors placed in my life by God, I still went to college and later graduated with academic honors from both college and seminary, was named "Student of the Year," and was the first African-American to graduate with a doctoral degree from Dallas Theological Seminary. But that was only because I had men speaking into my life at critical moments who helped me to get a glimpse beyond the sandlot and beyond my own limited perspective. These men helped me to believe in myself. They saw something in me even when I could not, which made all the difference in the world. Not just in my own life, but in my children's lives. And from the letters I get each week from listeners to my teaching ministry, it has made a difference in a number of people's lives as well, because I now have the opportunity to preach God's Word throughout the airwaves of America and around the world. Men you can make a difference in someone's life.

Down the Road

A portion of the conclusion of Psalm 128 talks about having a generational impact: "Indeed, may you see your children's children" (verse 6).

When a kingdom man orders his life to function personally under the lordship of Jesus Christ in his thoughts, will, actions, and prayers, that man's influence goes beyond himself and even beyond his own children to his children's children. That involves leaving a lasting legacy.

When my father, at the young age of twenty-nine, made the decision that he was going to place himself under Christ as the head over him, that he would love my mother according to the principles found in God's Word, and that he would raise us children according to the same principles, he not only affected himself, my mother, and us, but also his influence has reached to his children's children—and is continuing to reach to his children's children's children.

As I mentioned briefly before, I was born into a volatile home situation. My parents were on their way to becoming another divorce statistic when two men witnessed to my father and he trusted Christ for his salvation. Even though my mother did everything in her power to dissuade my dad from his newfound faith and life transformation, he was determined to fight for his family. He would wait until late into the night when she went to sleep to get out his Bible just so he could read without her complaining about it to him.

After several months of ordering his life as a kingdom man beneath Christ, my mom could not resist any longer. She came down the stairs with tears in her eyes ready and wanting to respond to what my dad had received in his life.

I was ten years old at the time. I am the oldest of four children and my father, a high school dropout, gathered all four of us around the table the next day to share the gospel with us. We also trusted Christ as our Lord and Savior. As I grew up, I watched my father consistently model responsibility, love, kindness, courage, and devotion to God. His life was a reflection of what a kingdom man ought to be. Because of my dad's encouragement, I became the first one in my family to ever graduate from high school. I was also the first one to ever go to college—let alone get a master's degree and later a doctoral degree.

My father's influence and impact gave me the foundation to start a church in my home with just ten people—albeit mostly relatives—which has now grown to over 9,000 and is centered on the core principles of God's kingdom. The church ministry also served as the foundation for our national ministry, The Urban Alternative, which broadcasts my messages daily in America and around the world.

All because of what happened to me when I was a kid—and because of the transformation I saw in my own life and family—I recognized the intersection that God provided when He brought the superintendent my way to ask us to get involved with the local public school. This then later served as a concept that former President Bush attributed as the impetus for his Faith-Based Initiatives Act when he first entered the presidency.

But none of that is about me. That's all about my father. Because when my father got saved and learned to fear God, he brought it home. When he brought it home, my mother became a fruitful vine and I became an olive plant at his table. He took us to Zion where I fell in love with the Word of God and sought to replicate that same love in my home with my own wife and children. So now when my father, who is in his eighties, turns on the television, he can sometimes see his grandson Anthony Jr. singing Christian music to the glory of God, even most recently as a witness for Him as a contestant on the secular television show *The*

Voice. Or he can flip to another Christian channel and see his granddaughter Priscilla Shirer teaching women's Bible studies all across America. Or when he visits Dallas, he sees his granddaughter Chrystal leading worship at church, or his grandson Jonathan serving in our local church or The Urban Alternative national ministry offices. This is all because when my dad got saved, he brought it home. Then he went to Zion. And now he sees his children's children taking the kingdom and advancing it to the next generation.

Even for the Fatherless

I understand that not everyone reading these pages is as fortunate as I was to have a kingdom man speak a covenantal blessing over me as a prince, a child of the King. I realize that many men grew up without a father or even a mentor in their life. Maybe you are one yourself. But God says He will be a father to the fatherless. Not only does He want you to learn and practice kingdom principles and mentor the next generation, but He also wants men who did not have the privilege of growing up under a kingdom man to intentionally

> *Our mission field is not merely across the sea. It is across the street.*

seek out someone in your local church or small group who can serve as this person in your life. That is what the body of Christ is about.

When we allow fatherlessness to continue at the rate that it is and do not take the necessary steps to change it, our society reflects it.

Our society's problem is not solely our government's problem. It is the church's problem. It is our problem. Our mission field is not merely across the sea. It is across the street—in our own Jerusalem and Judea—in Detroit, Dallas, Baltimore, Miami, and in your community. To look away now may cost us more than we can afford. It may even cost us the futures of our own sons and daughters.

Because of what God did in my own life through my father and through mentors He placed along the way, my heart is burdened to do the same for those in need. My heart is burdened to see men rise to the occasion within their churches and adopt local schools to be surrogate fathers to the fatherless. Through meeting social needs such as mentoring, tutoring, coaching, job training, and in countless other ways—we can tame this cultural chaos. We can reclaim our country for Christ.

In reaching the youth, we reach the families. In reaching the families, we reach the communities. In reaching the communities, we reach our nation. In reaching our nation, we reach our world. We need to do this before our world reaches us. As I mentioned before, over sixty percent of prisoners are high school dropouts. And over eighty percent of converts in prison convert to Islam.[5] In 2010, the number of Mosques in our nation more than doubled the number of Protestant megachurches.[6] Some schools send more kids to prison than to college.

Think about it. The threat to America isn't out there. The threat to our nation is within us.

The challenge we face is epic. The battle for morality, values, the family, the economy, education, health care, and our future is real. We need valiant men to step up and mentor the princes.

We need kingdom men who will change the world.

Before our world changes us.

This is not a time for secret agent Christians, spiritual CIA representatives, or covert operatives. The hour is too late, and the need is too great. It is time now for kingdom men to man up.

Everyone else is going public.

It is time for us as kingdom men to break our huddle and go public, too.

CONCLUSION

Barcelona, Spain, 1992. His name, before the race, brought little recognition or notoriety outside the island he called home.

Yet after the race, his name became known throughout the world as an icon of the spirit of the Olympics. His name stands for courage, determination, strength, perseverance, tenacity, character—and most of all, hope. In fact, as I write this conclusion some twenty years after this man ran, a petition is being circulated to have him light the cauldron for the next Olympics—which will be held, interestingly enough, in his native land.

His name is Derek Redmond. The race he is known for wasn't even a final, although he was favored to win a medal should he have made it that far. But he didn't. So he owns no Olympic medals at all. No world records either. In fact, he doesn't even hold a national record. But what Derek Redmond did when he ran that hot summer day in Spain impacted millions—both then and since—inspiring hope for when things don't end up like you had planned.

I'm sure you've seen the footage. Maybe you, like me, watched it live. Eight runners darting out of the blocks, angling around the curve. Redmond taking the lead after the first corner. Arms pumping rhythmically. Dreams hanging in the balance.

This was his time. And yet this was his tragedy as well.

Then—suddenly—Redmond grabs the back of his leg in what looks like excruciating pain. Hopping to a halt. Dropping to the ground on one knee. Next, laying flat on his back with the heat of the track scorching his soul. Tears of devastation forming in his eyes, threatening to betray how much he wanted to win this race. This was his race. This was his best chance at an Olympic medal. This was what he had trained for every day and every night for years leading up to the games.

This was his time.

And yet this was his tragedy as well.

As medical attendants made their way onto the track in an effort to help him off of it, Redmond saw them coming and, instead, struggled back up to his feet. In a frenzied effort to finish what he had started, he began hobbling in lane five. All eyes remained glued on Redmond as the look on his face revealed his agonizing pain. A security man tried to stop him, to reason with him, but Redmond fought through, pushing him aside. With all he had, Redmond fought to finish his race.

Yet 250 meters is a long way to go on just one good leg, even without a security man in your way. Each step became more difficult for Redmond. Soon his hobbling slowed down into hopping. And just when it looked like he could go on no longer, a large man in a ball cap and T-shirt raced down out of the stands. Tossing aside a member of security, he ran up behind Redmond and embraced him. It was Redmond's father.

The anguish on his son's face combined with the determination in his son's steps had made him come down to help. Putting his arm around him, he said, "We are going to finish this together."

Shortly before crossing the finish line, Redmond buried his face in his father's shoulder and went to wipe away his tears. Instead, his dad held Redmond's arm so that he could not do it. There was no reason to do it. What had started as tears of pain were now tears of determination. Nothing to hide. Tears of courage. Tears of two men fighting to finish what one had begun.

And they did just that. They finished.

Together, they finished the race.[1]

No, Redmond hadn't broken any record. And he certainly wasn't going to stand on any podium that night. But when Redmond crossed the finish line, all 65,000 spectators in attendance—as well as athletes and coaches and millions of viewers around the world—stood on their feet yelling, howling, cheering, some sobbing. In less than a minute, Redmond had become an international symbol and a household name.

This is because so many can identify with someone like Redmond. Maybe you can, too. You have set out to reach your goal only to have fallen short because of your own inadequacies, sinful rebellion, or paralyzing and crippling pain. People with good intentions try to help you off the track of your purpose and destiny. They tell you to take it easy. To settle. To move on. To let it go. Yet something within you won't let you forget the aspirations you held just around the corner in the starting blocks. And even though you once lay crumpled under the weight of unmet expectations, you somehow struggle to fight. Get back up. Hobble. Try. Daring someone to stop you even though you don't know how you could ever make it to the end on your own. Still, you fight.

I don't know what's been torn in your life, men, or what has left you injured—or even what you may have done to injure yourself through wrong decisions—making it so that you are not able to run as far and as fast as you should. Possibly you are not even able to get up from the track at all. But I do know the One who sees you. He will come down from on high to join you in lane five, if you will let Him. He knows your struggle. He knows your pain. If you listen, you can even hear Him say, "We are going to finish this together." Your heavenly Father stands ready to embrace you and help you cross the finish line as the victorious kingdom man He has destined you to be.

Your heavenly Father stands ready to embrace you and help you cross the finish line.

It is not too late. Your race is not over.

Get up. Push on through.

Fight.

Fight for your faith. Fight for your family. Fight for your church. Fight for your community. Fight for your nation. Fight for our world.

Fight for the finish line.

Fight.

And when you do, you will hear the deafening applause from heaven given for you, a kingdom man.

KINGDOM MAN
GAME PLAN SUMMARY

You can expand on this game plan summary by writing in your own specific goals.

Definition
A kingdom man is a man who visibly demonstrates the comprehensive rule of God underneath the Lordship of Jesus Christ in every area of his life.

Goal
To glorify God through the advancement of His kingdom by exhibiting responsibility and leadership in my personal, family, church, and community life.

Personal Life
To exercise responsibility in developing my spiritual, physical, intellectual, and emotional well-being and impact.

- Intentionally setting aside time to meet with God daily in His Word and through prayer for the purpose of cultivating spiritual intimacy, drawing down heavenly authority and receiving divine correction and instruction.
- Seeking to maintain optimal health and to maximize my mental and physical energy through regular exercise, eating a healthy diet, and getting an annual physical exam.
- Investing in my emotional, spiritual, and professional development through regularly reading books pertaining to my field or area of interest, listening or observing webinars, and attending conferences and/or seminars as possible.
- Carrying out fiscal responsibility in providing for my family, living within my means, paying down any existing debt (beginning with the smallest bill first), giving, and saving for the future.

- Exploring and discovering where my passion, experience, and greatest
  skills merge in order to then take increasing steps toward expanding
  the scope of my involvement and influence in those realms.

  _____

  _____

  _____

  _____

  _____

Family Life

To create an environment for my family to experience maximum satisfaction
and growth.

- Using the dinner table regularly for fellowship, discipleship, addressing
  the needs within the household, family devotions, and prayer.
- Regularly initiating and planning dates with my wife as well as daily
  communicating words of affirmation, and routinely setting aside time
  for in-depth communication.
- Developing with my wife an annual family budget that is reviewed
  together on a monthly basis, and developing with her a long-term
  financial plan that includes maintaining an updated will.
- Routinely modeling and teaching my children biblical principles of
  life issues regarding finances, relationships, faith, personal responsibility, goal setting, and more as well as investing in their lives through
  attending their events, reading to or with them, and actively engaging
  with them on a daily basis.
- Exposing my family to culturally diverse and enriching experiences
  to minister to, learn from, or engage with others from a different
  background.

  _____

  _____

  _____

  _____

  _____

Church Life

To be a contributing member of a biblically-centered church.

- Leading my family in weekly or bi-weekly church attendance as well as reviewing with them throughout the week what has been taught.
- Actively serving in a ministry that maximizes the use of my skills and gifts to help others.
- Regularly meeting with an accountability partner or partners in person and/or by phone for encouragement and authentic relationship.
- Financially investing in the ministry of my local church through tithes and offering.
- Intentionally engaging and mentoring those in my church without fathers.

_____

_____

_____

_____

Community Life

To tangibly contribute to the stability, progress, safety, and development of the community in which I live.

- Regularly sharing the gospel of Jesus Christ throughout my daily life.
- Joining with other men to arrange and participate in an event designed to reach and impact men in your city.
- Developing or participating in my church's community outreach ministry such as such as the National Church Adopt-a-School Initiative model program.
- Registering and voting for every election that affects my community.
- Investigating ways my gifts, skills, and/or business can contribute to the economic and social development of my community and/or a community nearby that is of lesser economic or social stability.

_____

_____

_____

_____

APPENDIX:
THE URBAN ALTERNATIVE

Dr. Tony Evans and The Urban Alternative (TUA) equip, empower, and unite Christians to impact individuals, families, churches, and communities for restoring hope and transforming lives.

TUA believes the core cause of the problems people face in their lives, homes, and society is a spiritual one; therefore, the only way to address the problems is spiritually. TUA has tried a political, a social, an economic, and even a religious agenda. Now it's time for a kingdom agenda—God's visible and comprehensive rule over every area of life. When the people of the church function as they were designed, divine power changes everything. It renews and restores as the life of Christ is made manifest within our own lives. As we align ourselves under Him, something happens from deep within—He brings about full restoration. He revives and makes us whole.

As the right alignment impacts us, it impacts others—transforming every sphere in which we live. When each biblical sphere of life functions in accordance with God's Word, the outcomes are evangelism, discipleship, and community impact. As we learn how to govern ourselves under God, we then transform the institutions of family, church, and society from a biblically based kingdom perspective. Through Him, we start touching heaven and changing earth.

To achieve TUA's goal, we use a variety of strategies, methods, and resources for reaching and equipping as many people as possible.

Broadcast Media

Hundreds of thousands of individuals experience *The Alternative with Dr. Tony Evans* through the daily radio broadcast playing on more than 500 radio stations and in more than forty countries. The broadcast can also be seen on several television networks and is viewable online at TonyEvans.org.

Leadership Training

The Kingdom Agenda Pastors (KAP) provides a viable network for like-minded pastors who embrace the kingdom agenda philosophy. Pastors have the opportunity to go deeper with Pastor Tony Evans as they receive greater biblical knowledge, practical application, and resources to impact individuals, families, churches, and communities. KAP welcomes senior and associate pastors of all churches.

The Kingdom Agenda Pastors summits progressively develop church leaders to meet the demands of the twenty-first century while maintaining the gospel message and the strategic position of the church. The summits introduce intensive seminars, workshops, and resources that address issues affecting the community, family, leadership, organizational health, and more.

The Pastors' Wives Ministry, founded by Lois Evans, provides counsel, encouragement, and spiritual resources for pastors' wives as they serve with their husbands in the ministry. A primary focus of the ministry are the KAP summits that offer senior pastors' wives a safe place to reflect, renew, and relax along with training in personal development, spiritual growth, and care for their emotional and physical well being.

Community Impact

National Church Adopt-A-School Initiative (NCAASI) prepares churches across the country to impact communities by using public schools as the primary vehicle for creating positive social change in urban youth and families. Leaders of churches, school districts, faith-based organizations, and other nonprofit organizations are equipped with the knowledge and tools to forge partnerships and build strong social service delivery systems. This training is based on the church-based community impact strategy from Oak Cliff Bible Fellowship. It addresses areas such as economic development, education, housing, health revitalization, family renewal, and racial reconciliation. NCAASI also assists churches in tailoring the model to meet the specific needs of their communities while simultaneously addressing the spiritual and moral frames of reference.

Resource Development

TUA is fostering lifelong learning partnerships with the people it serves by providing a variety of published materials. TUA offers booklets, Bible studies, books, CDs, and DVDs to strengthen people in their walk with God and ministry to others.

———

For more information, a catalog of Dr. Tony Evans' ministry resources, and a complimentary copy of Dr. Evans' devotional newsletter, call (800) 800-3222, write TUA at P.O. Box 4000, Dallas, TX 75208, or log on to TonyEvans.org.

NOTES

Chapter 1

1. *Strong's Greek Lexicon,* s.v. "*basileia,*" http://studybible.info/strongs/G932.

2. To read more on the "kingdom agenda," see the author's book *The Kingdom Agenda* (Chicago: Moody, 2006).

3. *Strong's Concordance,* s.v. "*Yahweh,*" http://concordances.org/hebrew/3068 .htm.

4. *Strong's Concordance,* s.v. " *'adown,*" http://concordances.org/hebrew/113 .htm.

5. *Strong's Concordance,* s.v. "*Jehova,*" http://concordances.org/hebrew/3068 .htm.

6. *Strong's Concordance,* s.v. " *'Elohiym,*" http://concordances.org/hebrew/430 .htm.

7. Sources for "Miracle on the Hudson," are as follows: USAirways.com, "US Airways flight 1549 transcript," http://www.usairways.com/en-US/about us/pressroom/1549_transcript.html; "Captain Chesley B. Sullenberger III," http://www.usairways.com/en-US/aboutus/pressroom/Sullenberger-bio.html; CBS News.com, "Flight 1549: A Routine Takeoff Turns Ugly," July 6, 2009, http://www.cbsnews.com/stories/2009/02/08/60minutes/main4783580.shtml; "Flight 1549: Saving 155 Souls In Minutes," July 6, 2009, http://www.cbsnews.com/stories/2009/02/08/60minutes/main 4783586.shtml; Fox News.com, "Surveillance Video Released of US Airways Plane Landing in Hudson River," January 17, 2009, http://www .foxnews.com/story/0,2933,480412,00.html; Kerry Burke, Pete Donohue, and Corky Siemasko, NYDailyNews.com, "US Airways airplane crashes in Hudson River—Hero pilot Chesley Sullenberger III saves all aboard," January 15, 2009, http://articles.nydailynews.com/2009-01-15/news/ 17914076_1_hero-pilot-air-force-fighter-crash-landed; Federal Aviation Administration, "INFORMATION: Full Transcript Aircraft Accident, AWE1549 New York, NY, January 15, 2009," http://www.faa.gov/data_ research/accident_incident/1549/media/CD.pdf.

8. Sources for "Tragedy on the Hudson," are as follows: CBSNews.com, "Newburgh mayor calls Hudson River deaths 'a tragedy,' " April 13, 2011, http://www.cbsnews.com/8301-504083_162-20053676-504083.html; Hudson Valley Insider, "Newburgh Mother and 3 Children Drown in Hudson River Tragedy," April 13, 2011, http://www.hvinsider.com/articles/newburgh-mother-and-3-children-drown-in-hudson-river-tragedy/; FoxNews.com, "Mother Drives Van Into N.Y. River, Killing Self and 3 Children," April 13, 2011, http://www.foxnews.com/us/2011/04/13/chief-mom-drives-ny-river-killing-3-kids/#ixzz1guzfiPOf.

Chapter 2

1. David Popenoe, *"Life Without Father," Mensight, Online Magazine of TheMensCenter.com*, (© 2000), http://mensightmagazine.com/articles/popenoe/nofathers.htm.
2. Raymond A. Knight and Robert A. Prentky, "The Developmental Antecedents and Adult Adaptations of Rapist Subtypes," *Criminal Justice and Behavior,* December 1987, vol. 14, 403–26 as quoted in The Fatherless Generation, http://thefatherlessgeneration.wordpress.com/statistics.
3. U.S. Department of Health and Human Services, Bureau of the Census, as quoted in Wayne Parker, About.com Fatherhood, "Statistics on Fatherless Children in America," http://fatherhood.about.com/od/fathersrights/a/fatherless_children.htm.
4. Cynthia Daniels, ed., *Lost Fathers: The Politics of Fatherlessness in America.* (New York: St. Martin's Press, 1998); National Fatherhood Initiative, *Father Facts* (Lancaster, PA: National Fatherhood Initiative, 1996); Elaine Ciulla Kamarck and William Galston, *Putting Children First: A Progressive Family Policy for the 1990s* (Washington: Progressive Policy Institute, 1990) as quoted in Stephen Baskerville, "The Politics of Fatherhood," © American Political Science Association, http://fathersforlife.org/articles/Baskerville/politics_fatherhood.htm.
5. Bill Whitaker, CBSNews.com, "High School Dropouts Costly for American Economy," May 26, 2010, http://www.cbsnews.com/stories/2010/05/28/eveningnews/main6528227.shtml#ixzz1PNhtcbfg.

6. C. Rouse, "Labor Market Consequences of an Inadequate Education," paper prepared for the symposium on the Social Costs of Inadequate Education, October 24, 2005, New York.

7. The National Campaign to Prevent Teen and Unwanted Pregnancies, "Counting It Up: The Public Costs of Teen Childbearing," http://www .thenationalcampaign.org/costs/.

8. Jennifer Warren, Pew Center on the States, "One in 100: Behind Bars in America 2008," February 2008, 5, http://www.pewcenteronthestates .org/uploadedFiles/8015PCTS_Prison08_FINAL_2-1-1_FORWEB .pdf.

9. Pew Center on the States, "One in 31: The Long Reach of American Corrections," (Washington, DC: The Pew Charitable Trusts, March 2009) 11, http://www.pewcenteronthestates.org/uploadedFiles/PSPP _1in31_report_FINAL_WEB_3-26-09.pdf.

10. Heartlight's Search Gods Words, *The New Testament Greek Lexicon*, s.v. "*ekklésia*," http://bible.heartlight.org/lex/grk/frequency.cgi?number=1577 &book=mt&translation=str.

11. Greek Dictionary.net, s.v. "*basileia*," http://www.greek-dictionary.net/ basileia.

12. *Strong's Concordance*, s.v. "*shamar*," http://concordances.org/hebrew/8104 .htm.

Chapter 3

1. Brett Martel, "Brees sets passing mark, Saints top Falcons 45–16" Associated Press, December 27, 2011, http://www.google.com/hostednews/ap/ article/ALeqM5jiXQRwoXv25PNTSBqAAxrjDypxCA?docId=02b1aa0e2 9d245a2a281e6629195cb8d.

Chapter 4

1. Wikipedia, "Hank Aaron," http://en.wikipedia.org/wiki/Hank_Aaron; Minor League Baseball.com, "Hank Aaron Stadium," ttp://web .minorleaguebaseball.com/team1/page.jsp?ymd=20090310&content_ id=522110&vkey=team1_t417&fext=.jsp&sid=t417; National Baseball Hall of Fame, "Aaron, Hank," http://baseballhall.org/hof/aaron-hank.

2. C. Brand, C. Draper, A. England, S. Bond, E. R. Clendenen, T. C. Butler and B. Lala, eds., *Holman Illustrated Bible Dictionary* (Nashville, TN: Holman Bible Publishers, 2003), 1474; J. E. Smith, *The Books of History*, Old Testament Survey Series (Joplin, MO: College Press, 1995), chapter 8.

3. IMDb, *The Matrix* (1999), http://www.imdb.com/title/tt0133093/.

Chapter 5

1. Frank Gifford and Peter Richmond, *The Glory Game* (New York: Harper Collins, 2008), 208-9.

2. Pro Football Hall of Fame, "National Football League Championship Game Play by Play, December 28, 1958," http://www.profootballhof.com/assets/history/58_Championship_PxP.pdf.

3. Jack Cavanaugh, *Giants Among Men: how Robustelli, Huff, Gifford, and the Giants made New York a football town and changed the NFL* (New York: Random House, 2008), 173.

4. Pro Football Hall of Fame, "National Football League Championship Game Play by Play, December 28, 1958," http://www.profootballhof.com/assets/history/58_Championship_PxP.pdf.

5. "Greatest game ever played," Pro Football Hall of Fame, http://www.profootballhof.com/history/release.aspx?release_id=1805.

6. Frank Gifford and Peter Richmond, *The Glory Game* (New York: Harper Collins, 2008), 217.

7. "Lenny Moore," Pro Football Hall of Fame, http://www.profootballhof.com/hof/member.aspx?PLAYER_ID=155.

8. Frank Gifford and Peter Richmond, *The Glory Game* (New York: Harper Collins, 2008), front flap copy.

9. Pro Football Hall of Fame, "National Football League Championship Game Play by Play, December 28, 1958," http://www.profootballhof.com/assets/history/58_Championship_PxP.pdf.

10. "NFL's All-Decade Team of the 1950s," Pro Football Hall of Fame, http://www.profootballhof.com/story/2010/1/16/nfls-all-decade-team-of-the-1950s/.

11. "Playoff Results: 1950s" Pro Football Hall of Fame http://www.profootballhof.com/story/2005/1/1/647/.

12. Dr. Kevin Leman, *The Birth Order Book: Why You Are The Way You Are* (Ada, Michigan: Revell Publishing, 2009) 22, 24.

13. Del Jones, "First-born kids become CEO material," *USA Today*, September 4, 2007, http://www.usatoday.com/money/companies/management/2007-09-03-ceo-birth_N.htm.

14. National Vital Statistics Reports, Vol. 59, No. 1, December 8, 2010, http://www.cdc.gov/nchs/data/nvsr/nvsr59/nvsr59_01_tables.pdf#tableI04.

15. Douglas W. Philips, *The Birkenhead Drill* (San Antonio, TX: The Vision Forum, 2001), 37, 39, 40, 24, 76; ElectronicScotland.com, "74th Highlanders: 1846–1853," http://www.electricscotland.com/history/scotreg/74th-2.htm; University of Wolverhampton, "Shared Heritage: Management of British Warship Wrecks Overseas," July 8, 2008, http://www.english-heritage.org.uk/publications/management-of-british-warship-wrecks-overseas/shared-heritage-management-of-british-warship-wrecks-overseas.pdf and The Queen's Royal Surreys Regimental Association, "The Birkenhead Disaster 26th February, 1852," http://www.queensroyalsurreys.org.uk/1661to1966/birkenhead/birkenhead.html.

Chapter 6

1. *Strong's Concordance*, s.v. "*bema*," http://concordances.org/greek/968.htm.

2. David Maraniss, *When Pride Still Mattered: A Life of Vince Lombardi* (New York: Touchstone, 1999), 274.

3. *Strong's Concordance*, s.v. "*kephale*," http://concordances.org/greek/2776.htm.

4. For an in-depth look at this and other issues related to marriage, see the author's books: *For Married Women Only* (Moody, 2010) and *For Married Men Only* (Moody, 2010).

5. All men are to be under the authority of the church leadership. A married woman is under the authority of her husband who in turn is under the authority of the church. A single woman is to be under the spiritual covering of the church since she has no husband, unless she is still living under the authority of her father (1 Corinthians 7).

6. For a more in-depth look at the study of the governing functions of the church, read the author's book titled *Oneness Embraced* (Moody Publishers, 2011).

7. W. Arndt, F. W. Danker, and W. Bauer, *A Greek-English lexicon of the New Testament and other early Christian literature*, third edition (Chicago: University of Chicago Press, 2000), 303.

Chapter 7

1. "Mammals: Jaguar," San Diego Zoo, 2011, http://www.sandiegozoo.org/animalbytes/t-jaguar.html; "Animal Bytes," San Diego Zoo, 2011, http://www.sandiegozoo.org/animalbytes/t-lion.html; Harrington, E. and P. Myers, "Panthera leo," 2004, (On-line), Animal Diversity Web. Accessed December 31, 2011 http://animaldiversity.ummz.umich.edu/site/accounts/information/Panthera_leo.html.
2. Jon Grinnell, "The Lion's Roar, More than Just Hot Air," *Zoogoer* (online), May/June 1997, http://nationalzoo.si.edu/Publications/ZooGoer/1997/3/lionsroar.cfm.

Chapter 8

1. *Strong's Concordance,* s.v. "*ezer,*" http://concordances.org/hebrew/5828.htm.
2. *Strong's Concordance,* s.v. "*kenegdo,*" http://concordances.org/hebrew/kenegdo_5048.htm.
3. *Strong's Concordance,* s.v. "*neged,*" http://concordances.org/hebrew/neged_5048.htm.

Chapter 9

1. *Strong's Concordance* s.v. "*shem,*" http://concordances.org/hebrew/8034.htm and *Strong's Concordance,* s.v. "*onoma,*" http://concordances.org/greek/3686.htm.
2. "Awards for Robert Duvall," The Internet Movie Database, 2011, http://www.imdb.com/name/nm0000380/awards.

Chapter 10

1. *Strong's Concordance* s.v. "*dynamis,*" http://concordances.org/greek/1410.htm.
2. *Strong's Concordance,* s.v. "*exousia,*" http://concordances.org/greek/1849.htm.

3. Steelers History, Steelers.com, "Super Bowl XLIII, Pittsburgh 27, Arizona 23," 2009, http://prod.static.steelers.clubs.nfl.com/assets/docs/Super_Bowl_XLIII_108708.pdf.

4. Greg Garber, "Holmes' grab secures Steelers' record sixth Super Bowl title," ESPN.com, http://scores.espn.go.com/nfl/recap?gameId=290201022.

Chapter 11

1. *Strong's Concordance,* s.v. "*darak,*" http://concordances.org/hebrew/1869.htm.

2. *Strong's Concordance,* s.v. "*epilambanomai,*" http://concordances.org/greek/1949.htmhttp://concordances.org/greek/1949.htm.

Chapter 12

1. *Strong's Concordance,* s.v. "*yare,*" http://concordances.org/hebrew/3373.htm.

2. *Strong's Concordance,* s.v. "*pusché,*" http://concordances.org/greek/5590.htm.

Chapter 14

1. *Strong's Concordance,* s.v. "*ekklésia,*" http://concordances.org/greek/1577.htm.

2. See Acts 19:39–41.

3. Deuteronomy 21:19–20; 22:13–19; 25:7–10, Joshua 20:4; 2 Samuel 15:2.

Chapter 15

1. *Strong's Concordance,* s.v. "Asher," http://concordances.org/hebrew/836.htm.

2. Bill Whitaker, CBSNews.com, "High School Dropouts Costly for American Economy, "May 26, 2010, http://www.cbsnews.com/stories/2010/05/28/eveningnews/main6528227.shtml#ixzz1PNhtcbfg; C. Rouse, "Labor Market Consequences of an Inadequate Education," paper prepared for the symposium on the Social Costs of Inadequate Education, October 24, 2005, New York.

3. Bob Smietana, "Statistical Illusion: New study confirms that we go to church much less than we say," April 1, 2006, http://www.christianity today.com/ct/2006/april/32.85.html.

4. "1.23 Million Students Will Fail to Graduate in 2008; New Data on U.S. Congressional Districts Detail Graduation Gaps: Graduation Data Available for Every U.S. School District and State," *Education Week*, June 4, 2008, http://www.edweek.org/media/ew/dc/2008/DC08_Press_FULL_FINAL.pdf; Robert Longley, "U.S. Prison Population Tops 2 Million," About.Com US Government Info Guide, http://usgovinfo .about.com/cs/censusstatistic/a/aaprisonpop.htm; Bill Whitaker, CBSNews.com, "High School Dropouts Costly for American Economy, "May 26, 2010, http://www.cbsnews.com/stories/2010/05/28/evening news/main6528227.shtml; K. Kost, S. Henshaw, and L. Carlin, "U.S. Teenage Pregnancies, Births and Abortions: National and State Trends and Trends by Race and Ethnicity, 2010," http://www.guttmacher.org/ pubs/USTPtrends.pdf; U.S. Government Census, "Table 78. Live Births, Deaths, Marriages, and Divorces: 1960 to 2008" and "Table 79. Live Births, Birth Rates, and Fertility Rates by Hispanic Origin: 2000 to 2008," http://www.census.gov/compendia/statab/2012/tables/12s0078 .pdf.

5. "Testimony of Dr. J. Michael Waller," United States Senate, Committee on Judiciary. October 9, 2003, http://judiciary.senate.gov/hearings/testimony. cfm?id=960&wit_id=2719 and http://homeland.house.gov/sites/homeland .house.gov/files/Testimony%20Downing.pdf.

6. The Pew Forum on Religion and Public Life quoted in Lauren Green, "Mosques Open Their Doors to Neighbors in Effort to Win Over Skep-tics," Fox News, October 22, 2010, http://liveshots.blogs.foxnews.com/ 2010/10/22/mosques-open-their-doors-to-neighbors-in-effort-to-win-over-skeptics/.

Conclusion

1. Rick Weingerg, "Derek and dad finish Olympic 400 together," ESPN.com, © 2009, http://sports.espn.go.com/espn/espn25/story?page=moments/94.

NOW MAKE
KINGDOM
MEN

Help empower the men in your church or small group to exercise the God-given dominion they were created for. Get the six-session Bible study based on this book.

www.lifeway.com/kingdomman

LifeWay | Men

FOCUS ON THE FAMILY®

Welcome to the Family

Whether you purchased this book, borrowed it, or received it as a gift, thanks for reading it! This is just one of many insightful, biblically based resources that Focus on the Family produces for people in all stages of life.

Focus is a global Christian ministry dedicated to helping families thrive as they celebrate and cultivate God's design for marriage and experience the adventure of parenthood. Our outreach exists to support individuals and families in the joys and challenges they face, and to equip and empower them to be the best they can be.

Through our many media outlets, we offer help and hope, promote moral values and share the life-changing message of Jesus Christ with people around the world.

Focus on the Family
MAGAZINES

These faith-building, character-developing publications address the interests, issues, concerns, and challenges faced by every member of your family from preschool through the senior years.

For More
INFORMATION

ONLINE:
Log on to
FocusOnTheFamily.com
In Canada, log on to
FocusOnTheFamily.ca

PHONE:
Call toll-free:
**800-A-FAMILY
(232-6459)**
In Canada, call toll-free:
800-661-9800

THRIVING FAMILY®	**FOCUS ON THE FAMILY CLUBHOUSE JR.®**	**FOCUS ON THE FAMILY CLUBHOUSE®**	**FOCUS ON THE FAMILY CITIZEN®**	
Marriage & Parenting	Ages 4 to 8	Ages 8 to 12	U.S. news issues	Rev. 3/11